THE UAHC
KIDS CATALOG OF
JEWISH LIVING

THE UAHC
KIDS CATALOG OF
JEWISH LIVING

Written and Illustrated by

Chaya M. Burstein

UAHC PRESS

NEW YORK, NEW YORK

Warm thanks to many people who have helped me to think through this text. To Bernard M. Zlotowitz and Michael A. Meyer for their thoughtful comments on ideas and facts; to Sim Gubitch, a teacher who can think like a kid; to Mark Shapiro and David Fine, Reform rabbis with zest; to Lisa, Amy, Sari, and Matt of BJBE; to Acum Ltd., Central Zionist Archives, Molly Cone, and photographers Ed, Dov, and Arieh for sharing their texts and photos with me; and finally to the hardworking editor, typesetter, and designer who struggled with a smudged and spliced manuscript.

Chaya M. Burstein

Library of Congress Cataloging-in-Publication Data
Burstein, Chaya M.
   The UAHC kids catalog of Jewish living/written and illustrated by
Chaya M. Burstein
      p. cm.
   Includes bibliographical references.
   Summary: A guide to living a meaningful Reform Jewish life,
exploring such aspects as Jewish history, holidays, prayers, and rituals.
   ISBN-0-8074-0464-0 (pbk : alk. paper) : $8.95
   1. Jewish way of life–Juvenile literature. 2. Jewish children–
United States–Religious life. 3. Reform Judaism–United States–
Juvenile literature. [1. Reform Judaism. 2. Judaism–Customs and
practices. 3. Ethics, Jewish.] I. Union of American Hebrew
Congregations. II. Title. III. Title: Kids catalog of Jewish living.
BM727.B87 1992   91-42815
296.7'4–dc20   CIP
                                                                  AC

Publication of this book
was made possible by a generous grant from the
AUDRE AND BERNARD RAPOPORT Library Fund

INTRODUCTION

Being Jewish happens accidentally to most Jewish kids. They are Jews because one or both of their parents are Jewish. But living as a Jew doesn't just happen. It takes some doing.

The big question is "doing what?"

Each person answers that question in his or her own way. But each thoughtful answer includes study of Jewish history and ideas, prayer, knowing about and enjoying Jewish holidays, and trying to be fair and caring with people.

This book will tell you more about the answers that Reform Judaism gives to "doing what?" It may help you to think of what you can do as a Reform Jew and why.

CONTENTS

Here are things that Reform Jewish kids do:

BELONG TO A TEMPLE

1

First, some background on temples.

THE FIRST TEMPLE

Solomon, king of Israel, built the First Temple about 3,000 years ago. It stood on a hill in the center of the Land of Israel. The city of Jerusalem grew up around it. Deep inside the Temple was a room called the Holy of Holies. Only the High Priest could enter it. This was where the Jews kept the ark that held the stone tablets of God's commandments.

In Jerusalem the holidays of Sukot, Passover, and Shavuot were like huge block parties. People came to the Temple dressed in their holiday clothing, bringing grain and fruits and young animals as gifts to God. The center of attention was the great altar in the Temple courtyard, where sacrifices were brought to God. As the smoke rose from the altar, the Temple musicians, the Levites, clashed their cymbals, banged drums, trumpeted, and piped on their flutes. Some people danced and sang. Other people gathered in groups to talk about the olive and grape harvests or argue about politics. Boys and girls flirted with one another, and parents arranged marriages. When the priests, the *kohanim*, finished offering the sacrifices, everybody feasted and celebrated together.

Nearly four hundred years later, Solomon's Temple was destroyed by an enemy army. Many Jews were driven into exile. The lonely, homesick exiles began to meet to help one another and to pray together. These meeting places may have been the first synagogues.

THE SECOND TEMPLE

When later some Jews were allowed to go home to the Land of Israel, they built a small Second Temple in Jerusalem, but they also continued to study together. About five hundred years later they enlarged the Temple and made it even more beautiful than the First Temple had been. The walls

The Talmud sages wrote: Whoever didn't see the temple of Herod (the king who enlarged the Second Temple) missed seeing the most beautiful building in the world.

were built of gleaming granite and marble. White marble columns covered with gold lined the courtyards and framed the giant altar. Fine mosaics, draperies, and bowls and candelabra of silver and gold filled the Temple. And again Jews came from near and far to worship and celebrate together.

After another fierce and bloody war, the Second Temple was destroyed in 70 C.E. Hundreds of thousands of people were forced to leave Jerusalem and the Land of Israel. With that tragedy the Jewish people sadly gave up on temples. There could be only one Temple, they thought—only the great Temple of Jerusalem. Until they could rebuild it in Jerusalem, they would have no Temple at all.

SYNAGOGUES

A legend tells that angels flew down from heaven when the great Temple in Jerusalem was burning. They swooped into the flames and lifted the stones of the Temple walls. Quickly they flew out over the world, dropping the stones here and there. Wherever a Temple stone fell a synagogue was built by the wandering people of Israel.

In new, strange lands Jewish exiles met to pray and study the Torah, the ancient scroll of laws and history that guided the Jewish people. Jews who were still in the Land of Israel met also. They called each of their meeting places a *bet knesset*, in Hebrew, or a synagogue, in Greek. Though they still arranged marriages, talked business, and sang prayers, they did not want musical instruments in the synagogue. How could they celebrate with loud, happy music when the great Temple, the house of God, was a heap of blackened, smashed stones!

Prayer took the place of sacrifice in the synagogue, and the *aron* or closet that held the Torah scrolls became a tiny Holy of Holies. Though they were scattered in many lands, the Jews still felt like one people. In most prayers, when they spoke to God, they used the words "we" and "us" instead of "I" and "me." Together they cried, "Hear us, O God!" The lost homeland of Israel was remembered over and over again in prayers and during the holidays of the Jewish year. To make sure that the community stayed united they decided that a group of at least ten men, a *minyan*, must come together for prayer in the synagogue.

The *minyan* was very democratic. Any Jewish man would do—whether he was an ignoramus or a scholar. A Yiddish proverb states: "Nine rabbis can't make a *minyan*, but ten shoemakers can." (A Reform *minyan* includes women.)

As the years passed, religious leaders explained and added to the laws of the Torah, helping Jews live by those laws in their new lands. Soon there were more and more laws and customs to learn. There were more prayers, too, because a prayer book or *siddur* was put together. The synagogue became the center of Jewish life. People met there to study Torah, to pray, to celebrate holidays and births, and to share one another's sadness when mourners recited the *Kaddish* prayer after a death.

REFORM SYNAGOGUES

Almost 1,800 years after the Second Temple was destroyed, a group of Jews in Germany decided to stop mourning and crying about the loss. They thought it was time to re-form Jewish ideas. They were happy in Germany. They wanted their prayers to relate to their new homeland rather than to the sad memories of the lost Temple and the lost Land of Israel. When the "Reform" Jews built a synagogue they called it a temple. They invited singers and musicians to make music in their temples. And men and women sat together, just as they had stood together long before in the outer courtyard of the ancient Temple in Jerusalem. (To learn about other changes made by the Reform Jews, see Chapter 4.)

Some things didn't change at all. For centuries the synagogues had been centers where Jews studied, prayed, and shared happy and sad times with one another. The temples of Reform Jews served their worshipers in the same way.

TODAY'S TEMPLES

Today there are 840 Reform temples in the United States. They come in many shapes and sizes. Some are built to look like tents, some like mountain tops, and some like colonial mansions. The most important room in every temple or *bet knesset* is the sanctuary, the room where people meet to pray. Here's how it is set up: On one wall, usually the wall facing Jerusalem, stands a carved and decorated closet, the *aron hakodesh*. It holds the greatest treasure of every temple, the Torah scrolls. Wrapped in soft velvet and wearing silver crowns and tiny silver bells, the scrolls are waiting to be taken out and read on holidays and on the Sabbath. (In traditional synagogues they are also read on Mondays and Thursdays.) In front of the *aron* is a platform or *bimah*, where the rabbi and cantor stand when they are leading services. The congregation usually sits in rows of seats facing the *aron*.

Joe Silberlicht

Did you know that people named Levy or Levine may have ancestors who were Levites, singers and musicians in Solomon's Temple, and people named Cohen, Kahn, and even Katz may be descended from the priests who served God in the Temple? All the rest of us are just plain Israelites.

The prayer service is very old and very young because it is always growing and changing. An example of "very old" is the Torah reading. Thousands of Jews—men, women, and children—stood together before the water gate of Jerusalem and heard the first public reading of the Torah (the Five Books of Moses) about 2,500 years ago. Torah reading has been part of prayer from the time of the earliest synagogues until today. Some of the prayers of the daily and Sabbath services are almost as old. When you stand up in the *bet knesset* to whisper the *Amidah*—the long, silent prayer—or to call out the words of the *Shema*—"Hear, O Israel..."—you can be sure that other Jews have been saying exactly these same words since the days of the ancient rabbis, after the destruction of the Second Temple. New prayers have been added over the centuries, and they are still being added. Prayers have also been dropped by some groups of Jews. So there isn't one *siddur*; there are several different ones—some thicker, some thinner. But each *siddur* contains basic prayers and the Torah reading service. When you read a traditional prayer, it is very likely that Jews in thousands of temples and synagogues from Tokyo to Brooklyn are speaking to God the same way as you are.

Someplace near the *bet knesset* in each temple is the social hall. Here parties and other big events happen. Sometimes the room rocks with ear-splitting music and shimmers with strobe lights for a bar or bat mitzvah party. Some days it's filled with hushed Scrabble or bridge fans. At Purim it jumps with skeletons, spacemen, Esthers, Hamans, and twirling noise-makers. Wedding parties, lectures, political rallies, fund-raisers—anything can happen in the social hall.

The education wing of the temple has classrooms for afternoon school or day school, a library, and often a nursery school.

Some large temples are Jewish community centers. The center may have a big kitchen in which to cook for parties, a gymnasium, a swimming pool, rooms for arts and crafts, and an outdoor ball field or playground. Jazzercize, adult study classes and lectures, ceramics, youth group activities, and giant book fairs may all become part of temple activities.

Some people ask, "Does all that stuff belong in a temple?" Others feel lost in a big temple. They want a small congregation so all the members can know one another and be friends. People who prefer small groups meet to worship in one another's living rooms or rent a small house to serve as a temple. They want enough room for prayers and study, a small religious school, and an electric coffee maker. Such a small group often calls itself a *chavurah*, the Hebrew word for "group."

In modern temples there is no awesome Holy of Holies; there are no sacrifices and High Priests and no pilgrims from across the world. The temples of today are very different from the two great Temples of ancient Jerusalem. But in some ways they are alike, aren't they? What do you think?

Activities

If you met an alien and he/she/it asked, "Wha-at isss a temmm-ple?" what would you answer? Fill in the voice balloon.

ABOUT YOU AND YOUR TEMPLE

What is the name of the temple you belong to? _____

If the name is in Hebrew, what does it mean in English? _____

What activities take place in your temple? _____

_____

Which do you take part in? _____

Which do other members of your family take part in? _____

What are three important purposes of a temple? _____

_____

How is your temple different from the Holy Temple in Jerusalem? _____

How is it the same? _____

INTERVIEW TEMPLE LEADERS

Talk to at least two temple officials such as the rabbi, cantor, principal of the religious school, director of youth activities, board members, presidents of the sisterhood and mens' club, etc.

Ask them to describe their jobs.

Ask them about new plans or ideas for the temple.

Suggest one new idea of your own.

MATCH IT

Draw a line connecting the related items in columns A and B.

A	B
1 Cohen	1 musician in the Temple
2 *minyan*	2 *siddur*
3 *bet knesset*	3 sacrifice
4 *Amidah*	4 *aron hakodesh*
5 Torah closet	5 Five Books of Moses
6 Torah scroll	6 silent prayer
7 *bimah*	7 temple or synagogue
8 altar	8 platform
9 prayer book	9 at least ten worshipers
10 Levite	10 priest in the Temple

Some Good Books

Freeman, Grace R., and Sugarman, Joan G. *Inside the Synagogue.*
   New York: UAHC, 1984.
Kuskin, Karla. *Jerusalem, Shining Still.* New York: Harper Collins, 1990.

JEWISH HISTORY

How do you explain Judaism? It's complicated. It's even hard to put into a category. You can't list Judaism under only R for religion or only H for history or only P for people. It is all of those things, all at the same time. To help understand Judaism and the reasons it has been going strong for more than 3,300 years, we'll start with a picture of Jewish history. Thirty-three hundred years won't fit into this chapter, not even into a fat book. But here are some high and low points, some ups and downs, from the time of Moses until today.

B.C.E. (before the common era) corresponds to the Christian B.C. C.E. (common era) corresponds to the Christian A.D.

1. About 3,300 years ago Moses led the tribes of Israel out of slavery in Egypt. At Mount Sinai they received the Ten Commandments and many other laws of God.

2. The tribes reached the land of Canaan, settled down, and became farmers. Each tribe was ruled by a judge, but they demanded a king to unite them into a nation. Saul and David were the first two kings of Israel.

3. The third king, Solomon, built the great Temple in Jerusalem in about 950 B.C.E. Priests brought sacrifices to God at the Temple. The people came to pray, bring gifts to God, and celebrate holidays.

4. After Solomon died the Kingdom of Israel split into two parts: Judea in the south and Israel in the north. Prophets struggled and argued to convince the kings and the people of both kingdoms to obey God's laws.

5. In 721 B.C.E. the northern kingdom, made up of ten tribes of Israel, was conquered. Its people were driven into exile and disappeared from Jewish history. Judea, the southern kingdom, too, was conquered about 134 years later. Solomon's Temple was destroyed, and many Judeans were carried off to Babylonia.

6. In Babylonia the Jews learned to practice Judaism without priests and without the Temple. They built synagogues, studied Torah, and prayed. Some Jews returned to Judea about fifty years later and rebuilt the Temple.

7. In about 300 B.C.E. the Syrian-Greeks captured Judea. More than a century later their king forced Jews to worship Greek gods. The Maccabees revolted and drove out the Greeks. For a short while Judea was independent.

8. The Romans conquered Judea in about 60 B.C.E. Jews rebelled again and again. In 70 C.E. the Romans burned the Temple to the ground and later drove the Jews out of Jerusalem.

9. Jews continued to live by the Torah's laws in Israel, Babylonia, and other lands. Scholars sat together, studied, and explained the laws. In about 500 C.E. the ideas and explanations were gathered into a large book called the Babylonian Talmud.

10. Christianity began and quickly spread in the Roman Empire. Jews were persecuted. Many left their land, which the Romans had named Palestine, and found homes in other countries.

11. A new religion called Islam was born in Arabia in 622 C.E. Arab armies carried it through the Middle East and neighboring lands. Jews often had freedom in Islamic lands. They became astronomers, doctors, poets, and philosophers.

12. Christian countries in Europe gathered armies to fight Islam. They called their wars the Crusades. Many Jews were killed by Crusaders during the eleventh, twelfth, thirteenth, and early fourteenth centuries.

13. When Spain became a Christian country, the oppression of Jews increased. The Inquisition tormented them and finally expelled them from Spain in 1492. Many escaped to North Africa, Italy, Turkey, and later to Holland and France.

14. A prosperous Jewish community grew in Poland. Jews were merchants and craftsmen. They built a strong religious framework based on *halachah* (Jewish law). Many Jews lived in walled-in neighborhoods called ghettos. In 1648 bloody pogroms shook the community.

15. A group of former Spanish Jews sailed from Holland across the ocean to the New World. In 1654 they settled in Niew Amsterdam, which later became New York.

16. The French Revolution and the Enlightenment freed Jews to leave the ghettos in western and central Europe in the early 1800s. Some Jews changed or reformed their religious practices to suit their new freedoms. In Eastern Europe a religious movement called Chasidism grew strong.

17. Many immigrants from Europe came to the United States in the mid-1800s. Some became peddlers and successful merchants. Among them were Reform Jewish immigrants. They built temples and their ideas began to spread.

18. Jews in Eastern Europe had a thriving Yiddish and Hebrew culture. They suffered increasing pogroms in the late 1800s. Many fled to the United States. A few went to Palestine to rebuild the Jewish homeland. They were called *chalutzim*, pioneers.

19. After World War One Great Britain received the mandate to help Jews build a national homeland in Palestine. In Germany the Nazi (National Socialist) movement was growing.

20. Nazi Germany attacked Poland and began World War Two in 1939. The Nazis imprisoned and murdered Jews in each country they conquered. During the war years one-third of the world's Jews, six million people, were killed in the Nazi Holocaust.

21. The British Mandate was ended and the State of Israel was established in 1948. While a bloody war for independence was being fought, Holocaust survivors and other Jews poured into Israel from all over the world.

Today one-half of the Jews of the world live in the United States. The second largest group lives in Israel. As the Jewish people prepare to step into the twenty-first century they can look back on more than 33 centuries of courage, faith, and terrible troubles. Shining 'UPS'. Tragic 'DOWNS'.

22. Since 1948 Israel has welcomed many immigrants. Ethiopian and Russian Jews are the most recent. The country has also fought five wars against its neighbors.

Activities

HISTORY REBUS

Solve the rebus and rearrange the letters to answer the following questions.

1. Which immigrants are coming to Israel today?
2. What's an early name for the Land of Israel?
3. What laws do Jews study and follow?

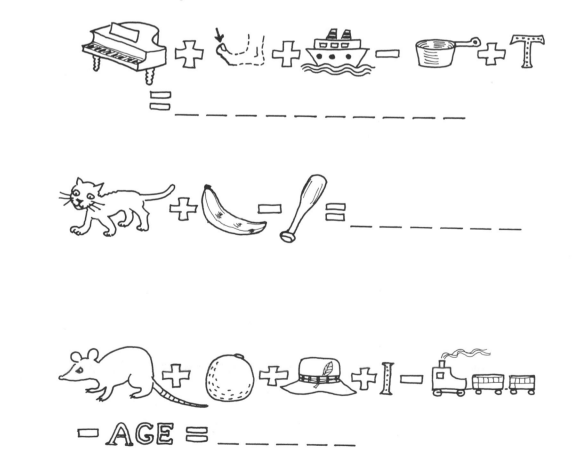

CHECK THE CORRECT BOX OR BOXES

1. At Mount Sinai the tribes of Israel received
   □ a special food called manna
   □ the Ten Commandments
   □ suntan lotion for the strong desert sun
2. People came to the Temple in Jerusalem to
   □ celebrate bar/bat mitzvahs and weddings
   □ bring gifts to God and celebrate holidays
   □ shop at the booths in the Temple courtyard
3. In Babylonia the Jews learned to
   □ pray and study Torah in synagogues
   □ eat falafel and pita
   □ build a strong Jewish community
4. After being driven out of Jerusalem, Jews wrote the Talmud to
   □ provide work for all the unemployed scholars
   □ adapt the Torah's laws to their changing lives
   □ explain the laws of the Torah more fully
5. Under Christian and Muslim (believers in Islam) rulers, Jews
   □ lived peacefully and shared the local customs
   □ were often persecuted and killed
   □ developed a strong Jewish religious framework, a *halachah*
6. For centuries many Jews lived in ghettos, which were
   □ an ancient section of Rome
   □ large, fancy houses
   □ Jewish neighborhoods surrounded by a wall
7. The Enlightenment brought to the Jews of western and central Europe
   □ electric lights for each home
   □ freedom to leave the ghettos
   □ Chasidism
8. Many Jewish immigrants came to the United States in the 1800s to
   □ find economic opportunities and become rich
   □ escape from pogroms and anti-Semitism
   □ find religious freedom
9. The word "Holocaust" describes
   □ a huge, terribly destructive fire
   □ the murder of six million Jews by the Nazis during World War Two
10. The people of the State of Israel
   □ come from all over the world
   □ are all Holocaust survivors
   □ are of different religions

Some Good Books

Adler, David A. *We Remember the Holocaust*. New York: Holt, 1989.
Burstein, Chaya M. *The Mystery of the Coins*. New York: UAHC, 1988.
Bush, Lawrence. *Rooftop Secrets and Other Stories of Anti-Semitism*. New York: UAHC, 1986.
Eisenberg, Azriel; Goodman, Hannah Grad; and Kass, Alvin, eds. *Eyewitnesses to Jewish History*. New York: UAHC, 1972.
Ish-Kishor, Shulamith. *A Boy of Old Prague*. New York: Scholastic, 1979.
Ofek, Uriel. *Smoke over Golan*. New York: Harper and Row, 1979.
Roseman, Kenneth. *The Cardinal's Snuffbox*. New York: UAHC, 1982.
_____. *Escape from the Holocaust*. New York: UAHC, 1985.

JUDAISM'S HOLY BOOKS

3

The highlights of Jewish history make it seem as if Jews had been running from country to country for hundreds of years, suffering pogroms and struggling to stay alive. Was it really like that? If it was, how could they live through it? Why did they stay Jewish? Why are we here today?

To answer those questions, imagine that you are in a strange place. Pretend that you went on an overnight hike. You hiked all day. In the evening you unrolled your sleeping bag in a dark forest and crawled in. But you were too cold and scared to sleep. You shivered and listened to the whine of mosquitoes, the creaking branches of trees, and the rustle of wild animals in the bushes. Snakes, bears, man-eating lions! Would morning ever come? Only the orange flames of the campfire kept you warm and safe. You prayed the fire would last till morning.

During the hardest years of Jewish exile from the Land of Israel Jews must have felt like campers huddled around a fire in a dark forest. They heard howls and roars and thrashing in the bushes. Dangerous enemies surrounded them. Only the glowing fire kept them safe. They could even sing and tell stories in the dark because they knew that the night would end and the forest would become green, sunny, and friendly.

THE TORAH

The glowing fire at the center of Jewish life was the belief in God and the Torah. The customs that grew from the Torah have filled Jewish life with satisfying ceremonies, holidays, and religious duties. Most important, Torah has given Jews the hope that the night would end and that all people would accept God's law. Then the whole world would be happy and peaceful.

The Bible is an all-time best-seller. Two and a half billion copies have been printed in 275 languages.

These Jews of Yemen had only one book of Torah. They sat in a circle when they studied, and they learned to read upside down and sideways as well as right side up.

Central Zionist Archives

Torah has come to mean all of Judaism's holy books, beginning with the *Tanach* or Bible. The Torah, the scroll we read in the temple, is the first of three sections of the *Tanach*. The Torah is called the Five Books of Moses; in Hebrew it is called the *Chumash*. It describes the creation of the world; the stories of Adam and Eve, Noah, Abraham, Moses–the great teacher of the Jewish people; and more. It also contains an agreement between God and the Jewish people that the people will obey God's laws and God will protect them and help them to become a powerful nation.

The other two sections of the *Tanach* or Bible are called Prophets and Writings. Prophets tells about the Temple in Jerusalem; the kings of Israel; and the stormy, God-fearing prophets. One of those prophets called on the Jewish people to be a moral light, a guide to all other peoples. Love songs like the Song of Songs and cliff-hanger stories like the tale of Purim are found in Writings.

The *Tanach*, the Temple, the kings, the priests, and the prophets unified and guided the people while they lived in their own land. But when they were driven into exile they lost everything except the Torah (the *Tanach* and other religious lore). Would it be enough to guide them in far-away lands?

WRITTEN AND ORAL TORAH

In those strange lands new questions came up each day. Here are some examples of such questions:

The Torah says we may not light a fire on Shabbat. Does that mean we have to sit in the dark and freeze on a winter Shabbat day?

What does the Torah mean when it says, "Don't boil a young goat in its mother's milk"? Can I boil a potato in milk? Can I serve chicken with ice cream?

The Torah says we should take an eye for an eye and a tooth for a tooth. Should we poke out the eye of a person who accidentally pokes out somebody's eye? What if that person has only one eye? What if the person is blind?

Now that our Temple is destroyed we can no longer bring sin offerings to God. How will God forgive our sins?

Rabbis and teachers had to answer these and many other questions. They met to study the ancient Torah scrolls, the Written Torah. In the written words they searched for hidden meanings that would provide answers. The meanings that they found were called Oral Torah because at first they were not written down. They were only discussed and remembered. But how much can people remember, even wise rabbis and teachers? After a while, the new ideas were collected in a book called the *Mishnah*. After 300 more years of discussion, another book called the *Gemara* was written. The *Mishnah* and *Gemara* together are called the Talmud.

WRITTEN AND ORAL

The following story from the Midrash tells about two servants. They represent the Jewish people. Each servant was given raw wheat and flax—just as the Jewish people were given the Written Torah. Only one of the servants used the materials to make bread and cloth—just as only some of the Jews used the words of the Written Torah as a basis for the further study and teaching that became the Oral Torah.

The Midrash asks: What is the difference between the Written Torah and the Oral Torah?

Compare it to a king who had two servants. He gave each one a bundle of flax and a bag of wheat. One servant spun the flax and wove it into cloth. He ground the flour, kneaded it, and baked it into bread. Then he spread the cloth on the bread and left it for the king.
  The other servant did nothing.
  When the king returned, he said, "My sons, bring me what I gave you."
  The servant who had done nothing was ashamed and disgraced.
  When God gave the (Written) Torah to Israel, God gave it to us as wheat—for us to make bread and flour—and as flax—for us to make cloth.

Adapted from the Talmud, *Seder Eliahu Zuta*

More books were written over the years as scholars pushed and pulled the words of the Torah and Talmud to keep their basic meanings safe but to adapt them to new conditions. For example, here are answers that were found for the questions you read earlier:

Shabbat laws were clarified so that there could be light and warmth (and hot chicken soup) in Jewish homes on the Shabbat, although Jews would still not light fires.

The laws of *kashrut* (keeping kosher) were expanded to set clear rules that separated dairy, meat, and parve (neither meat nor dairy) foods and utensils.

The "eye for an eye" law was explained to mean that a fine must be paid to the victim.

Instead of bringing a sin offering to the Temple, Jews could pray sincerely to God and repent for their sins.

The word "Torah" has several meanings. It is the scroll we read in the synagogue—the *Chumash*. It is also the books of *Chumash*, Prophets, and Writings—the *Tanach*. According to Jewish tradition, God gave the *Chumash* to Moses on Mount Sinai. It is the Written Torah. As other Jewish holy books were written, Torah began to include them also. They are called Oral Torah. Some Jews use the word Torah to mean all the writing that is important in the life of a Jew.

Proverbs 3:18 calls the Torah "a tree of life" to those who hold it close. The tree keeps growing as Jews find new meanings in their religion and write them into new books. On this page is a picture of the tree of Torah with some of the writings that have formed its branches over many years.

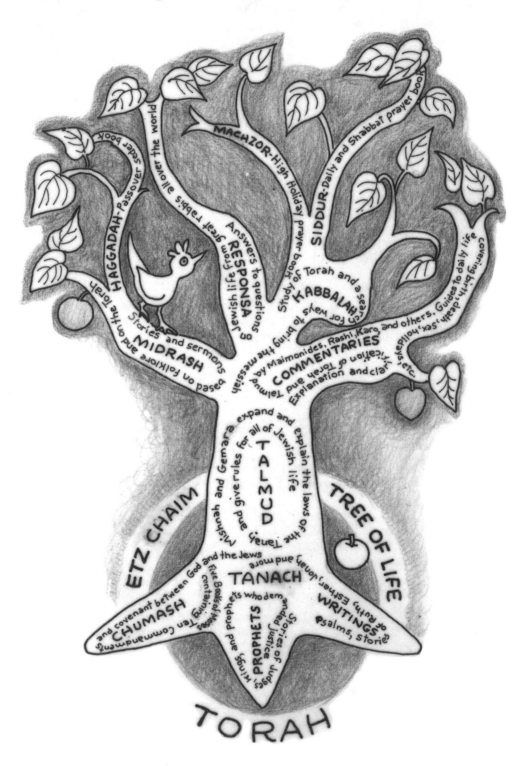

WHY ARE JEWS HERE TODAY?

Let's get back to the questions of why Jews stayed Jewish and why we are still here today. In the Torah God gave the Jews an important purpose: They are to live according to God's laws and be an example to other people so that, sooner or later, all people will draw close to God and peace will come to the world.

Okay, so Jews have an important purpose and they have their law, the Torah. Is that what kept them going through the hard times of Jewish history? Earlier in this chapter we called the Torah the glowing fire at the center of Jewish life. It is surely the hottest part of the fire, but there's also a warm outer circle of flame. This outer circle is the Jewish way of living. It is Jewish holiday celebrations, prayer and study, stories, jokes, special foods, a feeling of closeness and sharing with other Jews, a proud history, a tie to Israel, caring about others, and more. The next chapters will tell about our way of living as Reform or Liberal Jews.

This Yiddish lullabye shows how important Torah study was for European Jews.

RAISINS AND ALMONDS

Under my little child's cradle   My child will study Torah.
A pure white goat stands.   A rich man my child will become,
The goat will go to market   And a good pious Jew he will always be.
To sell raisins and almonds.

Activity

ADVICE FROM OUR FATHERS

How should we behave toward one another . . . when can we ignore somebody's troubles . . . do we always take care of Number One (ourselves) first? The Talmud gives good advice in a section called Sayings of the Fathers.

Check the sayings that seem right to you.
Choose one and describe a situation where you would use that advice.
☐ Do not judge your comrade until you have stood in his or her place.
☐ It is not your duty to finish (all) the work, but you don't have the right not to do any of it.
☐ Be a tail to lions rather than a head to jackals.
☐ If I am not for myself, who will be for me? If I am only for myself, what (good) am I? And, if not now, when?

_____

_____

_____

_____

Some Good Books

Burstein, Chaya M. *The Hebrew Prophets*. New York: UAHC, 1990.
Freehof, Lillian S., and Schwartz, Howard. *Bible Legends: An Introduction to Midrash*. Vols. 1 and 2. New York: UAHC, 1987, 1988.
Rosman, Steven M. *Sidrah Stories: A Torah Companion*. New York: UAHC, 1989.
Rossel, Seymour. *When a Jew Seeks Wisdom: The Sayings of the Fathers*. New York: Behrman House, 1975.

4

THE BEGINNINGS OF REFORM JUDAISM

IN A COMFORTABLE RUT

The Jews of Europe had been stuck in a rut for centuries. They were allowed to work in only a few trades such as money lending and selling used merchandise or junk. They could live only in certain cities or areas of each country. Even in those areas, they had to live in Jewish neighborhoods called ghettos.

In some ways it was a comfortable rut. People lived close to one another and to their schools and synagogues. They studied Torah together, celebrated holidays, and followed the rules of *halachah* (the way to go) drawn from the Talmud. *Halachah* directed their lives from morning until night. Men and boys wore old-style clothing that looked different from the clothing of non-Jews. Everybody spoke Yiddish or Ladino—their own languages. And they had as little as possible to do with the unfriendly, non-Jewish world.

From time to time, that world burst in on them. Mobs of non-Jews would pour through the ghetto gates screaming, "The Jews killed our Lord, Jesus! Kill the Jews!" They would smash windows, steal, burn houses, beat people, and sometimes kill them. When the mobs left, loaded with loot, the people of the ghetto would sadly bury their dead, mend the windows, and return to their work, their prayers, and their customs.

In the early 1800s, nearly 200 years ago, new ideas of freedom and equality began to change western and central Europe. Many harsh laws were dropped and the gates of many ghettos were opened. In countries like Germany and France, Jews opened businesses, studied at the universities, and lived wherever they liked. To be free was wonderful, but it caused certain problems.

PROBLEMS WITH FREEDOM

Jews looked in the mirror and saw their beards and earlocks, their black coats, *kipot*, and broad-brimmed hats. Some were embarrassed. Nobody else dresses like this, they thought. Shears clicked and the beards and earlocks disappeared. Tailors stitched new ruffled shirts and trim velvet jackets and knee pants. Now a modern Jew looked like everybody else.

Religious laws made problems, too. If Jews ate only kosher food, they could not have dinner with their new, non-Jewish business acquaintances. If they observed the Shabbat, they couldn't open their stores on Saturday when all the other stores were open. And they couldn't travel to trade fairs on holidays.

Even the synagogue service was a problem for modern Jews. They felt that it was not orderly and dignified. Families didn't sit together. The women had to sit behind a screen on an upstairs balcony. The men sat below, around the reading platform. Some worshipers swayed over their prayer books, some prayed aloud, some discussed business or the latest news, and children scrambled in the aisles. Prayers sounded sing-song rather than melodious. And, when it was time to read the Torah, the men bid noisily against one another for the honor. The richest bidder won. Some people could not feel close to God in the hectic atmosphere of the synagogue. Others stopped coming because they were embarrassed by the disorder. Many Jews even turned away from their religion and converted to Christianity.

In those early years of 1800 it seemed that Judaism was a delicate plant that could grow in the dark ghetto but would shrivel and die in the strong sunshine of freedom. "Not so!" cried Orthodox Jews. They believed that the customs of traditional Judaism were God's law. It was the only true Judaism and, if it had survived the ghetto, it surely would survive in the free world.

A second group of Jews cried "not so" but for a different reason. They accepted the moral laws of Judaism and many of its traditions. But they believed that some Jewish traditions were old-fashioned, like "a garment from a different time and place." "Judaism has always adapted its traditions to changes in Jewish life," they said, "and now it must reform its traditions, adapt to freedom, and grow strong."

RE-FORMING JUDAISM

In 1801 a German Jewish merchant named Israel Jacobson took a daring first step toward reform. He started a school for poor Jewish boys that was different from the traditional religious school. In the traditional schools the boys studied Hebrew, Torah, and Talmud, but in Jacobson's school they studied not only religious subjects but also farming and trades. Then, even more daringly, Jacobson accepted girls (who had usually gotten no schooling) and non-Jewish students as well. Some years later the determined Jacobson built a synagogue. Christians and Jews attended the opening service on a July morning in 1810. It may have been the first interfaith service in history! And it was not a traditional Jewish service. There were organ music, choral singing, a sermon in German, and prayers in both Hebrew and German. Everybody present behaved politely, recited

Do not limit a child to your learning, for he was born in another time.   Rabbinic saying

Here's what some early Reform rabbis said:

Wherever you are treated humanely, wherever you prosper, there also is your Palestine, your fatherland, which in accordance with your [Jewish] law you must love and defend.   David Frankel

The Talmud speaks out of the consciousness of its age and for that time it was right. I speak out of the higher consciousness of my age and for this age I am right.
                Samuel Holdheim

The Greeks have a talent for sculpture, the Romans have a talent for law, and the Jews have a genius for religion.   Abraham Geiger (Geiger explained that Christianity and Islam had grown from Judaism, and he believed that Judaism could again be a source of religious growth and change for Jews and for all humanity.)

prayers in unison, and agreed that the new temple was a great success. But other Jews fought against Jacobson's reforms and complained to the government. The school struggled with many problems and survived until the Nazis came to power in Germany.

The problems of being Jewish in the world of the 1800s would not disappear. More and more young Jews lost interest in their religion and became Christians. Jewish parents tried desperately to work out religious practices that would have meaning for their families. One effort in 1845 was very successful. A group of Jews met in Berlin to "establish Judaism in a form in which it will be able . . . to live on in us and in our children." They decided to celebrate the High Holy Days in an exciting, new way. On Rosh Hashanah eve the prayer hall was packed with people. Many more had to be turned away. Jews who hadn't been in a synagogue in years came. They hoped to find a prayer service that would feel right to them. Here are some of the things they did:

Both men and women sat on the main floor.

Most men were bareheaded, without hats or *kipot*.

The prayer book was shortened to forty-eight pages and written in German with only a few lines of Hebrew.

The *shofar* was not blown in the morning because people found the sound too harsh and disturbing.

The rabbi's sermon was a central part of the service.

Does this sound wildly radical to you? In the 1800s they were thought to be radical changes, which delighted a few worshipers and made many others very angry.

Temples that followed some of these Reform ideas were founded in Germany and Austria. The new ideas were discussed, fought about, and shaped by lay people and by such rabbis as Abraham Geiger and Ludwig Philippson. Gradually Jews in England, France, and other European countries were drawn to Reform. Rabbis rewrote traditional prayer books into shorter texts without a lot of repetition. Temples were built in a new design with the reading desk in front of the ark instead of in the center of the room, without a screened-off women's section, with a choir loft for singers, and with an organ.

ABRAHAM GEIGER (1810-1874)

American Jewish Archives

Two very different rabbis of the Breslau synagogue stood by a newly dug grave. One was old, bearded Solomon Titkin, an Orthodox Jew who believed that the laws of the Torah and the Talmud were God-given and unchangeable. The other rabbi, Abraham Geiger, was young and clean-shaven, with long hair pushed back behind his ears. Geiger was a historian and Bible scholar who believed that Judaism's holy books had changed even as they were being written. He thought that modern Judaism must continue to change and adapt to its environment.

Both rabbis were to speak in honor of an important congregation member who had just been buried. But most of the "mourners" didn't seem to be thinking about the dead man. They were gathered in separate groups around each rabbi, glaring at each other.

Rabbi Titkin made his speech in peace. When it was Geiger's turn, his opponents started to shout insults. Geiger's supporters shouted back. The shouting grew louder and louder across the clumps of raw, brown earth. Then somebody punched somebody else. Soon everybody was punching and scuffling. Finally the police came clanging into the cemetery to separate the battlers.

After the cemetery battle the congregation split into two: a Reform congregation and an Orthodox congregation. The split made Geiger sad. During his whole life as a rabbi he wrote books, delivered sermons and speeches, and tried to draw the whole Jewish community toward a broader view of Judaism. The spirit of Judaism, derived from the holy books, is what binds Jews together, he explained. The ideals and faith of the prophets are the eternal elements of Judaism. Individual traditions can be changed, but the spirit and ideals are eternal.

Geiger faced great opposition and never united his people. But he hammered out an ideology of Reform Judaism that is still basic to Reform beliefs today.

REFORM VERSUS ORTHODOX

As Reform ideas spread, the separation between Orthodox and Reform Jews grew wider and wider. Orthodox Jews did not want changes in customs and rituals. To them the organ became a hated symbol. A group of Hungarian rabbis proclaimed that to pray in an "organ temple" was as bad as eating pork. Reform leaders were disappointed. Once they had hoped to draw all Jews together into a modern Judaism that would suit the free, open world of the 1800s. But that hope died as most Jews continued to accept only traditional Judaism based on traditional *halachah*. The ideas of Reform Judaism influenced traditional Jewish practices but didn't replace them. Reform became a new and separate branch of Judaism.

Then came another disappointment: the happy time of freedom and equality began to end in western Europe. By 1850 harsh new laws oppressed both Jews and non-Jews. As a result, many people packed up and left the Old World. Reform Jews went along with the others. In the United States they hoped to build a secure home and communities where they could practice their Judaism in freedom.

Activities

BATTLE LINES

In the 1800s Orthodox and Reform Jews often argued.

Do you know who thought what?

Draw a line connecting each statement to the correct voice balloon.

The Torah does not tell Jews to cover their heads. No *kipah* for me!

Our Holy Temple is destroyed. There should be no musical instruments in our synagogue.

Only the Torah is holy. The rulings of Talmud, etc., are people's opinions, and we can change them to suit our times.

We must pray for the Messiah to come to bring us back to Israel.

A land where we are well treated is our homeland. We don't need to pray for the Messiah to bring us to the Land of Israel.

Men and women should sit and worship together. And both boys and girls should have religious education and confirmation.

Hebrew is our holy language–the only language for Jewish prayer.

Men and women have different roles in religious life. Torah study is more necessary for men than for women.

Hebrew is a beautiful, ancient language, but people should pray in the language they speak and understand.

Jews must cover their heads out of respect for God.

Musical instruments were used in the Temple.

We can use them in our synagogue.

WHAT DO YOU THINK?

Why did some German Jews decide to reform their religious practices in the early 1800s?

_____

_____

_____

What changes did they make?

_____

_____

_____

REFORM JUDAISM IN THE UNITED STATES

5

LAND OF OPPORTUNITY

German Jewish immigrants walked down the gangplank into an exciting, wide open world. In the mid-1800s Americans were bumping across the country in covered wagons to claim homesteads. A lucky few were becoming instant millionaires, finding gold in California. Some trudged country roads selling needles, cloth, and frying pans while dreaming of becoming rich storekeepers. And some, like Adam Gimbel, made it! It was a land of opportunity. Anything could happen.

Religious life was wide open because the United States Constitution promised religious freedom. Many Americans did not feel tied to the old European churches. They formed new Christian sects and sang, shouted, and talked to God in new ways. Reform Jews felt at home. The United States was moving forward, not looking back. Their Judaism could be part of this movement.

Rabbi Isaac Mayer Wise came to the United States in 1846 with a grand dream. He wanted to unite Reform and traditional Jews in a progressive movement of American Judaism. His chances looked good. Reform Jewish ideas were spreading quickly to cities like Charleston, Baltimore, New York, Albany, and Cincinnati. There were organs and mixed choirs in the temples, and men and women sat together at services. But traditional Jews stayed with the traditional customs. And there were arguments even among the Reform Jews.

ISAAC MAYER WISE (1819-1900)

It took a warm, people-loving, energetic, and learned man to organize American Reform Jews into a single, large movement. Rabbi Isaac Mayer Wise had all those qualities.

American Jewish Archives

Wise was the son of an Orthodox Hebrew school teacher in Bohemia. When he came to the United States at age twenty-seven he had great plans. He was determined to bring the traditions of Reform Judaism to all the Jews of America. But he started out by getting into trouble with his first congregation. He explained that he didn't believe in a personal Messiah or in resurrection of the dead. The outraged president of the synagogue tried to throw him off the *bimah*. A few years later Wise found a friendlier pulpit at Temple Bene Yeshurun in Cincinnati, Ohio. It became his base for the next forty-six years while he built the American Reform movement. But, even as he worked to strengthen the Reform movement, Wise kept trying to unite traditional and Reform synagogues. For the sake of unity he was ready to ease some of his religious ideas. Other Reform rabbis, including David Einhorn, refused. They wanted no compromises.

Wise's great plan of unity failed. But he led the Reform congregations to form their Union (UAHC) and then to found the first successful rabbinic college in the United States, Hebrew Union College. Rabbi Wise became president and chief professor. In between teaching classes this tireless man wrote novels, lectured, traveled, led his congregation, wrote a widely used prayer book, and organized countless conferences.

One of his opponents said glumly, "He defines the course of American Judaism . . . he has succeeded, and nothing is as successful as success."

ARGUING AND GROWING

David Einhorn, a rabbi in Baltimore, was a fierce believer in classical Reform as it was practiced in Germany. He thought Wise was a compromiser who would give up liberal Reform principles just to gain support from non-Reform Jews. In the angry years before the Civil War, Einhorn declared that slavery was a religious, moral issue, and it was a cancer eating away at the nation. Some Jews who lived in the South were for slavery. They demanded that Jewish leaders should not take a stand. But Einhorn kept speaking loudly and strongly against slavery. He finally had to run for his life just before the pro-slavery townspeople of Baltimore came to tar and feather him.

After the Civil War, the domes and towers of new temples popped up in many cities. Soon there were more temples and synagogues than rabbis, and congregations wanted American rather than immigrant rabbis. For once, traditional and Reform Jews worked together to solve the problem. In 1873 they set up the Union of American Hebrew Congregations (UAHC) and in 1875 the Hebrew Union College (HUC) in Cincinnati to prepare young men to become rabbis. It seemed as though Isaac Mayer Wise's dream of a united American Judaism was coming true. But, only a few years later, the dream was drowned in a platter of shellfish. The non-kosher food was served at a party for the first HUC graduating class. Some guests were insulted and furious at the "*treyfe* (non-kosher) banquet." Two years later, in 1885, the traditionalists were upset again when they read a new statement of Reform principles called the Pittsburgh Platform. This time even Wise couldn't mend the broken partnership. Traditional Jews left the UAHC and HUC to form their own Conservative movement.

Hebrew Union College started in 1875 with one teacher and nine students in a small building in downtown Cincinnati. Since 1912, teachers and students have enjoyed this building.

THE PITTSBURGH PLATFORM

The Pittsburgh Platform was a hopeful, upbeat statement of the ideas of classical Reform Judaism. It looked forward to a better world that Jews would build along with others. Judaism with its advanced ideas of God would continue to be a separate religion, and Jews would be a priest people, as stated in the Bible. But they were no longer a nation and did not expect to return to Palestine. They would observe only the Jewish moral laws and ceremonies that made sense in the modern world. Old rules about clothing, food, etc., were no longer useful.

You might think that the Pittsburgh Platform would have cleared things up and that Reform Jews could finally settle down and follow their own style of religion. But that didn't happen. There were too many questions left unanswered. Should rabbis marry Jews to non-Jews? How much Hebrew should there be in the services? Should we blow a *shofar*, a trumpet, or nothing at all? Should there be Sunday, Shabbat, or Friday night services? Do Jews have a religious responsibility to help poor people, mistreated workers on strike, and fighters for women's rights, etc? In 1895 there was a sign of unity. Most Reform temples accepted a revised *siddur* called the *Union Prayer Book*. It left out some traditional prayers and reflected the ideas of the Pittsburgh Platform.

As years passed the American Jewish community began to change. Once a majority had been immigrants from Germany. Many had wholeheartedly supported Reform ideas. But in the late 1800s thousands of immigrants began to arrive from Eastern Europe. They brought with them a love of Jewish traditions that classical Reform Jews had pushed aside. Many were also Zionists who felt that the Jewish people should have their own homeland.

Eventually people of Eastern European background began to join Reform temples, and slowly the temples began to look and sound different. Purim masquerade parties and Chanukah candlelightings were introduced. Families began to demand bar mitzvahs. These celebrations became as important as the confirmations, sermons, and harmonious choir music of classical Reform.

By the 1930s Reform Jewish leaders knew they had to rewrite the fifty-year-old Pittsburgh Platform to suit their changing community.

> Reform responsa were intended to provide guidance, not governance.
> Solomon Freehof

RABBI MARK REMEMBERS . . .

Grandma Lena was an enthusiastic "*davener.*" In her very proper Reform temple she and her grandson, Mark (today Rabbi Mark Shapiro), would pray along with the rabbi and hum with the cantor. This annoyed some of the other worshipers. One Friday night when the choir and Grandma Lena took off on a rousing *Adon Olam*, a neighbor leaned over and hissed, "Ssssh! Don't sing! The choir is singing." Grandma Lena took a deep breath, glared at her neighbor, and announced, "I'm gonna sing, and so is my grandson!" *Adon Olam* never sounded better, Mark remembers.

THE COLUMBUS PLATFORM

The Columbus Platform of 1937 declares that belief in God is the heart of Judaism, and the Torah is the basis of Jewish life. People in each age must adapt Torah teachings to their needs. Prayer is the voice of Jewish religion in the home and in the synagogue. As Jews we also need Hebrew, Shabbat, and other festivals and customs. We are loyal citizens of our countries, but we also must help build the Jewish homeland in Palestine. For Jews religion and morality work together. We strive for justice and the end of war, prejudice, and inequality.

Columbus in 1937 sounded different from Pittsburgh in 1885. It talks about building a homeland in Palestine, enjoying holidays and customs, and fighting prejudice and inequality. Morality and adapting Torah to each age are important, as they were in Pittsburgh, but with Hebrew, holidays, and direct social action Jews now have more to *do* and more to enjoy.

WAR AND HOLOCAUST

World War Two began in 1939. For six years it raged and tore the world apart. By the time it ended, one-third of the Jews of the world—six million people—had been killed by the Nazis and their helpers. The Holocaust left an aching hole in Jewish life. Germany, the birthplace of Reform Judaism, was emptied of Jews. Eastern Europe, the warm center of Jewish culture, was a graveyard. Jews asked themselves how God could have allowed this horror to happen. No answer satisfied everyone, but all Jews agreed that the only way to finally defeat Nazism was to make Judaism strong and vital again. America and Israel would become the new, living centers of world Jewry.

CHANGES

After the war, many young American Jewish families moved from the cities to the suburbs. The trees and grass were nice, but they were lonely. Grandma's and Grandpa's house with chicken soup and family get-togethers was faraway. They wanted a Jewish connection. New Reform temples were built in the suburbs to provide prayer services, religious schools, sisterhoods, men's clubs, and youth groups.

More changes followed. Young rabbis and cantors played guitars at jazz services. Women studied to become rabbis at Hebrew Union College–Jewish Institute of Religion. Reform lay people and rabbis joined civil rights marches and anti-Vietnam War demonstrations. Passover seders, Shabbat candlelighting, and other traditions became regular parts of Reform Jewish home and temple life. Increasing numbers of Jews-by-choice (converts) joined Reform temples. And people worried about Israel and worked to support it. In 1968 rabbinic students began to spend their first year of study in Israel. A new *siddur* called *Gates of Prayer* was written in 1975. It allowed for traditional prayers in alternative services. With all these changes it was time to review Reform principles again.

A CENTENARY PERSPECTIVE

In 1976 the Central Conference of American Rabbis (CCAR) wrote *A Centenary Perspective: New Platform for Reform Judaism*. The Reform rabbis who wrote it faced some difficult issues. They were reacting to the tragedy of the Holocaust, to the relationship of Reform Jews to the State of Israel, and to divisions within the Reform movement itself. They began by pointing out that many Reform Jewish ideas have been accepted by other Jews. Then they went to the bases of their faith: the belief in God and belief in the Torah as both a heritage and a living, growing tradition. Religious belief is important, they stressed, but prayer, study, and Jewish practices are the primary expressions of Jewish life. Jews are responsible to work for a better world but they are also to be devoted to the survival of their own people. Jews support and feel linked to the State of Israel. In spite of the tragedy of the Holocaust, Jews have hope that people can affect their own destiny and help to create a better world.

Today there are Reform Jewish temples all across the United States, from Hollywood, California, to Bangor, Maine. They don't all look or sound the same because there is no rigid Reform practice or *halachah*. But tradition was carefully considered in the writing of Reform's standard prayer books and the guide books to holiday celebrations, life-cycle traditions, and prayer.

If David Einhorn and Isaac Mayer Wise skipped ahead 120 years and came to a Shabbat service at your temple, it would astonish them. Einhorn would shudder to hear rock melodies used with some prayers. Wise would cluck, "tch, tch, tch," at the loud singing–so noisy and undignified. If you were to have a woman rabbi they would probably be pleasantly surprised. But, if she gave an enthusiastic sermon about the State of Israel, they would protest indignantly.

American and Jewish life has changed in many ways since those two rabbis stepped off the ship from Germany in the mid-1800s. But Wise and Einhorn would have to agree that one principle of Reform Judaism has remained the same: Judaism is a living, growing religion. It holds tightly to its belief in God and the moral standards of Jewish law, and at the same time its traditions develop and change with the changing lives of the Jewish people.

"*Gott in himmel!*" Rabbi Einhorn might say to Rabbi Wise as they leave the Temple. "What will the year 2000 bring?"

Other names for Reform Judaism are Liberal Judaism or Progressive Judaism. The Israeli name is a mouthful! It is *Tenuah li-Yahadut Mitkademet*, the Movement for Progressive Judaism.

WORLD UNION FOR PROGRESSIVE JUDAISM (WUPJ)

Most Reform Jews live in the United States, but there are others all over the world. Reform Jews live in cities as widely scattered as Moscow, Buenos Aires, Melbourne, and Hong Kong. Since 1926 there has been a World Union for Progressive Judaism to which most Reform communities belong. Its headquarters are now in Jerusalem, Israel. Through the World Union strong Reform congregations are able to help new or weak congregations. The World Union sends rabbis to work with Jews in the Soviet Union and is helping a young Russian to study for the rabbinate in England. When he goes home he will be the first native-born Reform rabbi in the Soviet Union. Special projects including scholarships to study are sponsored for communities in Central and South America and elsewhere. Har Halutz, a tiny Reform settlement in Israel, is receiving help to bring interested Russian immigrants to the settlement. New, small congregations all over the world who can't afford to pay a rabbi are helped by the World Union.

"All Jews are responsible for one another," says the Talmud. WUPJ gives us one way to carry out that responsibility.

Rabbi Leo Baeck was a leader of the World Union. He lived through an awesome and tragic time in Jewish life. As a young man in Germany he was a respected scholar and community leader who wrote and lectured on Judaism and the nature of God. "Begin to create the future!" he cried out hopefully to Jews in the 1920s. He demanded that Jews take their religion seriously and struggle to make the world a better place.

Only a few years later Nazism rose in Germany, and the world became unbelievably worse instead of better. As Nazi persecution of the Jews became more vicious, Baeck took the difficult job of representing German Jews to the Nazi government. At the same time he headed the World Union for Progressive Judaism, the organization of Reform Jews in many lands.

By the time World War Two burst out in 1939 the German Jewish community had disappeared into Nazi prisons and concentration camps. In 1943 when Leo Baeck was seventy years old, he was sent to the Theresienstadt concentration camp. Though other prisoners died or were deported all around him, Baeck somehow lived through the war and saw the defeat of Nazi Germany. And then, with courage and energy, he picked up where he had left off . . . struggling to make the world a better place.

Again Rabbi Baeck took up the leadership of the World Union for Progressive Judaism and lectured throughout the United States. His message was, "Begin to create the future!"

Rabbi Leo Baeck

Activities

Below are names and dates associated with Reform Judaism. Use the first letter of each word in the name to do this crossword puzzle. In 5 Across, spell out the whole name.

ABC OF REFORM JUDAISM

Across
  1. Central Conference of American Rabbis began in 1889
  5. First headquarter city of Reform Judaism in the United States
  8. Reform Judaism
  9. Union of American Hebrew Congregations, 1873
 10. National Federation of Temple Brotherhoods, 1923
 11. National Association of Temple Educators, 1954

Down
  2. Association of Reform Zionists of America, 1977
  3. Hebrew Union College, 1875
  4. Jewish Institute of Religion, 1922
  6. National Federation of Temple Sisterhoods, 1913
  7. World Union for Progressive Judaism, 1926
 10. North American Federation of Temple Youth (formerly National Federation of Temple Youth), 1939

Now write the crossword puzzle number for each name next to the description of its work.
_____   Association of Reform rabbis that sets policy on social and religious issues and prepares educational material
_____   Organization of Reform women who raise money to support Hebrew Union College, help at temple functions, etc.
_____   Reform Jews who actively support Israel and Reform settlements and institutions in Israel
_____   The religious movement of Reform Judaism

_____ Schools at four campuses for study of Jewish education, sacred music, and preparation for the rabbinate

_____ Association of high-school age boys and girls who meet to have fun, learn about Jewish issues, and apply *mitzvot* to daily life

_____ Organization of Reform men who organize adult education and social projects and help at temple functions

_____ Union of Reform Jewish congregations that sponsors camps, seminars, educational material, etc.

_____ Association of Reform Jewish principals, teachers, and other educators

_____ Organizations of Reform Jewish congregations throughout the world

A Good Book   Meltzer, Milton. *The Jews in America: A Picture Album.* Philadelphia: Jewish Publication Society, 1986.

THINK ABOUT GOD AND SPEAK TO GOD

6

It used to be simple to think about God. In ancient times, each country had its own gods. Everybody could see or feel these gods. There were gods of nature like the sun or moon gods, and there were idols or statues that people made. These gods were very touchy. They would get angry for no good reason, and then–watch out! Locusts might come and eat your harvest, the rain might stop falling, or all the kids might get chicken pox at the same time. People pampered their gods by building fancy temples for them and bringing gifts and sacrifices (even human sacrifices) to keep them happy, friendly, and well fed.

When you moved to a new land, you switched to the new gods because your old gods had no power outside their own territory. If a strong king conquered your country, you brought gifts to his gods. After all, your old gods were losers. Why stay with them? Simple and logical.

But the God of the Hebrews didn't follow that logic. First God made a covenant with Abraham and his descendants, the Jewish people. Later God turned up in Egypt, which wasn't his turf at all by the standards of the time, and helped the Jewish slaves to escape. Then, from a cloud atop Mount Sinai, the Almighty made another agreement with the Jewish people, which was written in the Ten Commandments and the Torah. They were not to make idols or to worship other gods–not ever, not anyplace! They were to bring gifts and sacrifices (not human sacrifices) to the Hebrew God. But that wasn't enough–they must also be just and kind with one another. They were to be a chosen people living by God's rules, an example to all other people. And, if they did right, God would make of them a mighty nation living in peace in its own land.

Phew! Those rules were hard enough to keep while the Jews lived in the Land of Israel. It became even harder when they were forced to leave. The Temple was burned to the ground along with its secret Holy of Holies. Who could they pray to? And where? What was God? How could God and the Jewish people relate to each other in new, strange lands? Over the years, in many different countries, Jews asked and answered these questions. We still ask them today.

WHAT IS GOD?

There are no photos or fingerprints of God to help answer this question. Each person has his or her own answers. Here are some of them:

> The artist Michelangelo, who read in the Bible that people were made in God's image, decided to paint God as a strong, wise-looking man with a long, white beard.

> The writer Molly Cone wrote: God is a Presence that is everyplace in the universe, just as water is everyplace in the sea.

This is Astarte, the Canaanite goddess of love and fertility. She was carved about 2,500 years ago.

To love God truly you must first love people. And if anyone tells you that he loves God but does not love his fellow human beings, he is lying.   Chasidic saying

39

Rabbi Joshua Loth Leibman wrote: God is all the creativity and love that is within us.

The sage Sa'adia Gaon wrote: There is nothing that resembles God.

It was also said: God is a guiding force with reason and purpose that makes sense of the world—even though we humans may not understand how or why.

What do you think?

WHERE IS GOD?

Where is God?

What does God look like?

Sometimes we wish we could find answers to these questions.

Molly Cone told about a little fish with a similar question. He learned that water was important, and he wanted to find it. "Where is water?" he asked fish after fish. No one could tell him.

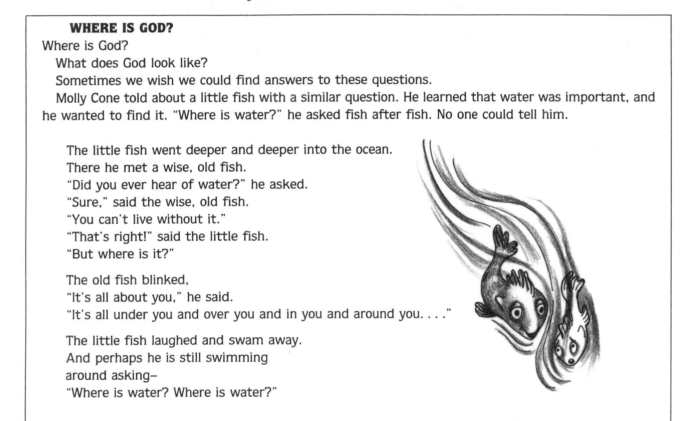

The little fish went deeper and deeper into the ocean.
There he met a wise, old fish.
"Did you ever hear of water?" he asked.
"Sure," said the wise, old fish.
"You can't live without it."
"That's right!" said the little fish.
"But where is it?"

The old fish blinked,
"It's all about you," he said.
"It's all under you and over you and in you and around you. . . ."

The little fish laughed and swam away.
And perhaps he is still swimming
around asking—
"Where is water? Where is water?"

Where is God? A Jewish prayer answers the question with the words: "Holy, holy, holy, the whole earth is full of God's glory."

Excerpted from *Hear, O Israel: About God* by Molly Cone

HOW CAN GOD AND THE JEWISH PEOPLE RELATE TO EACH OTHER?

Sometimes the Torah describes God as a shepherd and the Jewish people as God's flock of sheep. Sometimes God is a judge who passes judgment on the people. In both these examples God is a high, powerful force who guides and judges us.

The Bible and the *siddur* (prayer book) call God the Creator of all living things and give God's message in these words: "Look, today I am offering you life and good things or death and bad things." God is telling us that the Torah sets rules by which we should live. The way we choose to live can help make the world better or it can add to the ugliness and cruelty

The world is new to us every morning–this is God's gift. And every person should believe he is reborn each day.

Ba'al Shem Tov, founder of the chasidic movement

in the world. It's up to each of us. In this example, God is still high above, challenging us to run our lives properly.

But some Jews see the relationship between God and the Jewish people as a partnership. We need God and are responsible to do God's will, but God also needs us. After all, if *we* don't follow God's laws, who will? And, if nobody does, how will God's work in the world be done? So God must hold up one end of the partnership by being fair in dealing with us.

The following story tells how the chasidic Rabbi Levi Yitzhak of Berdichev reminded God of this partnership:

> On Yom Kippur eve Reb Levi Yitzhak noticed that Jacob the tailor was not in the synagogue. The rabbi sent the sexton to call him, but Jacob replied that he would not come—not until God apologized. Levi Yitzhak was shocked. He himself went to Jacob's house and asked, "Why should God apologize?" The tailor told him this story:

> He, Jacob, had been out of work for a long time. There was no food in the house and no money for his daughter's dowry. Suddenly he was called to the house of the local nobleman and given furs to make a fur coat. Jacob was very happy. He would be paid for his work, and he would at least be able to buy food. But things turned out even better. He finished the coat perfectly, and he had a few bits of fur left. The nobleman can't do a thing with these little pieces, he thought, but I can make some fur hats to sell, and I'll earn the money for my daughter's dowry. He hollowed out the two big loaves of bread he had brought, hid the fur inside, and started out for home. Suddenly he heard the pounding of horse's hooves behind him. In a panic, he thought that the nobleman was chasing him and would punish him for taking the fur. He quickly tucked the stuffed bread under a bush.

When the nobleman's servant reached Jacob, he explained that the nobleman wanted some buttons sewn on his new coat. With a sigh of relief, Jacob went back to sew the buttons. Then he returned to the bush . . . and found the bread and the furs were gone!

"I know who took the furs!" Jacob exclaimed to Levi Yitzhak. "It was God. He was trying to teach me a lesson. But this time God is not right. *I'm* right. And I'm not coming to synagogue until God apologizes!"

Levi Yitzhak persuaded the angry tailor to stand at the rear of the synagogue. Then he went up to the *aron hakodesh* and stood facing the Torah for long, long moments. He swayed with his head bent, as if he were praying and listening. At last he straightened up and turned with a shining face. "Jacob," he called, "go and get your *machzor* and *talit*. God apologized!"

Adapted from a story by I.L. Peretz

IS THERE A GOD?

There are people who suggest, "Maybe there is no God. Maybe the whole universe grew by chance, and the Torah was made up by human beings."

It's difficult to imagine how things as beautiful and complicated as a butterfly, a baby, and a thundering volcano could have happened just by chance. And it's hard to imagine a world that grew without any purpose or guidance. Babies struggle to walk because they imitate their brothers, sisters, or parents. Painters work when they are inspired by a sunset or a clump of flowers. We all need a reason to reach higher and higher. And we need to feel part of a world that has meaning and purpose. God's teachings offer the goals, the meaning, and the purpose.

Some people disagree. "Where was God's meaning and purpose when six million Jews died in the Holocaust?" they ask. "Why is a baby born with AIDS? Why is a little child on a tricycle killed by a hit-and-run driver?"

There are no good answers to those questions. We can't find valid reasons for the terrible things that happen. We only know that we have been given a green, fertile world, and some human beings have done murderous things to it and in it. We need strength to turn things around. Belief in God and prayer can help give us strength and show us the right direction.

ABOUT PRAYER . . . SPEAKING TO GOD

When the Jewish people lost their Temple, they could no longer speak to God with gifts and sacrifices. They could speak only with prayer. Synagogues were built wherever Jews lived. The ark with the scrolls of Torah became a tiny Holy of Holies. And people met in the synagogue to study Torah, to pray, and to share their joys and worries with God and one another. Prayer was in Hebrew. It is the language of the Torah, and Jews everyplace in the world know at least a little Hebrew.

The prayer service has evolved over hundreds of years. It follows the order of the sacrifices in the Temple with a morning service called *Shacharit*, an afternoon service called *Minchah*, and an evening service

Where is God? Wherever you let God in.
There is no room for God in those that are full of themselves.
From *Gates of Prayer*, the Reform prayer book

called *Ma'ariv*. *Shacharit* starts with happy psalms that tell of the wonders of God who is praised by the mountains and hills, the trees of the forest, the kings, and the people. Every living thing cries "Hallelujah!"

Included in all three daily services are the two oldest prayers in the *siddur* (prayer book): the *Shema* and the *Shemoneh Esreh* or *Amidah*. "Hear, O Israel, the Lord our God, the Lord is One!" cries the *Shema*. It calls to us to accept God's commandments and obey them. At the saddest times in Jewish history, when Jews were killed because of their religion, they cried the words of the *Shema* with their last breaths.

The *Amidah* is a longer, silent prayer. Traditionally, we stand and say the words to ourselves. We praise God and ask God's help to become better, wiser people. We pray for health, prosperity, peace, the coming of redemption, and more. One by one people finish reading and sit down. In the whispering silence they add their own private words to God.

On Shabbat, Monday, and Thursday we can take the beautifully dressed Torah scroll out of the *aron*. The silver decorations sparkle and the little bells ring as the Torah mantle and crown are lifted off. Then we unroll the scroll to the section of the week, *parashat hashavua*, and congregation members are called up to the *bimah* for an *aliyah*. They say the blessing over the Torah and read from the scroll or have somebody read for them. This is important because Jews believe that when they pray they speak to God and, when they hear the words of the Torah, God is speaking to them. On Shabbat and holidays it is customary also to read from the section of the *Tanach* called Prophets. For a bar or bat mitzvah this section becomes his or her special reading.

Another daily prayer is the *Kaddish*. Its words praise and glorify God, and it has become a prayer in which we remember family members and others who have died. The *Kaddish* ends with the hope, "May God who makes peace in the high heavens make peace for us and for Israel."

The rabbi and cantor are leaders and guides for the congregation during the synagogue service. On Shabbat and holidays the rabbi gives a sermon that may explain parts of the Torah reading or may tie religious and moral ideas to our daily lives.

Why are there bells on the Torah mantle and crown?

So that their ringing should wake up sleeping worshipers in time for the Torah reading.

Speaking to God in prayer is always important, but it becomes a special *mitzvah* when Jews pray together as a group. Jewish prayers speak of "us" and "we," the people of Israel, rather than of "I" or "me." The Talmud says: "Those who pray with the congregation shall have their prayers granted. Why? Because worshipers who pray with their fellow Jews are praying not only for themselves but for the good of all."

Jews pray at home as well as in the synagogue. And they say many blessings, *berachot*. On Shabbat there are blessings over the candles, the wine, and the challah. There are blessings to be said when we get up in the morning or see a bright rainbow or eat a new kind of fruit or light a Chanukah candle. For every good thing that happens, we can stop and say a blessing, a "Thank You" to God. The blessing adds a sense of wonder to every simple thing we do—from washing our hands to planting a tree.

So what does prayer do for us? Can it get you a new bike or a bigger allowance? No. But prayer gives us time to listen to ourselves and also to try to hear what God wants of us. It can help us to get a broader view of what is important in our lives and in the world around us. And prayer in the temple helps us to feel close to other worshipers so that we understand and care about one another.

A PRAYER
Dear God, please help me to get up. I can fall down by myself.
Yiddish saying

Activities

What do you think about God? Where is God? What qualities do you think God has?

_____

_____

_____

_____

List four characteristics of God that you find in the *siddur*.

1.   2.   3.   4.

CAN YOU MATCH THESE?

Draw a line connecting these prayers, services, and songs with their meanings.

1	*Hatikvah*	1	evening prayer service
2	*Kaddish*	2	morning prayer service
3	*Shemoneh Esreh*	3	going up to the Torah
4	*berachah*	4	Torah reading of the week
5	*Shema*	5	Hear, O Israel
6	psalms	6	afternoon prayer service
7	*parashat hashavua*	7	praising the wonders of God
8	*aliyah*	8	*Amidah*, a prayer said while standing
9	*Shacharit*	9	anthem of the State of Israel
10	*Minchah*	10	prayer praising God as we remember the dead
11	*Ma'ariv*	11	blessing

BERACHAH

"Thank-You" prayers or blessings begin with "*Baruch Atah Adonai...*" (bless You, God...). Write a "*Baruch Atah...*" of your own about something for which you are especially grateful.

_____

_____

Kushner, Lawrence. *The Book of Miracles: A Young Person's Guide to Jewish Spirituality.* New York: UAHC, 1987.   **A Good Book**

7 RIGHT AND WRONG

Do right! Be fair! Protect the underdog!

These words have echoed in Jewish ears since the first meeting with God. It happened in the gray desert at the foot of Mount Sinai about 3,300 years ago. Thunder rumbled, lightning slashed through the darkness, and the earth shook as the awe-struck Jews listened to God's commandments. Many laws came thundering from the mountaintop, but among the first were laws to protect the weak–the slaves, the women, and the strangers. "You shall not oppress a stranger," God ordered, "because you were strangers in the land of Egypt."

COMMANDMENTS ARE FOR EVERYONE

Why did God create only one Adam, and all races sprang from him?

So that no one could say: My father is better than your father.
Talmud

Years passed. The Jews were no longer trembling ex-slaves. They were farmers and merchants with their own land, Temple, and king. But God's commandments didn't change. Even the kings of Israel weren't free to be bullies and tyrants like other kings. King David ignored the commandments when he fell in love with Bathsheba, the wife of another man. He sent Bathsheba's husband off to war to be killed and then married her. The prophet Nathan blasted David for his sin and God punished David for what he had done. King Ahab, who loved fresh vegetables, stole a vineyard from one of his subjects (over the subject's dead body) and turned it into a vegetable garden. The king and his wife, Jezebel, were punished, too.

Later prophets like Amos and Micah demanded that the leaders of Israel follow God's laws by taking care of their people and behaving justly rather than by trying to bribe God with fat sacrifices. The prophet Isaiah put an even heavier burden on the people and their leaders. "It is not enough that you restore the people of Israel," Isaiah spoke in the words of God. "I will also make you a light for the nations, so that My salvation may reach to the ends of the earth."

The Jewish people were driven out of Israel sometime after Isaiah's prophecy. With the pogroms, expulsions, and persecutions that they suffered during the centuries of exile, they had trouble just helping one another stay alive. The saying from the Talmud–all the people of Israel are responsible for one another–had more immediate meaning than Isaiah's plea that they be "a light for the nations."

No one is lonely when doing a *mitzvah* because a *mitzvah* is where God and man meet.
Abraham Joshua Heschel

COMMITTEES AND MORE COMMITTEES

Long before Social Security and unemployment insurance, Jews formed groups to help one another. In every town there was a committee to provide schooling for orphans and poor children, another to collect dowry money and provide wedding dresses for poor brides, and another to arrange shelter for travelers and homeless people. There was a society to visit the sick, a society to prepare the dead for burial, and a fund to rescue Jews who had been taken captive or sold into slavery.

During happy celebrations people remembered to give charity. The poor were given *matzah* and wine at Passover, money at Purim, and donations after a wedding or a *brit*. A lucky traveler who escaped a shipwreck or a wagon wreck rushed home to say a prayer of thanks and give a gift to the poor.

Life changed when the ghettos opened up. Many Jews entered the non-Jewish world. They felt safe and grateful for their new freedom. Early Reform Jews began to think about their responsibility to all people as well as to the Jewish community. When they wrote the Pittsburgh Platform of Reform principles in 1885, they expressed Isaiah's idea in these words: ". . . to solve, on the basis of justice and righteousness, the problems presented by the . . . evils of the present organization of society."

Worshipers slip coins into the hands of this charity box. It stands in the entrance hall of a synagogue in Prague, Czechoslovakia. The Hebrew words mean "A gift in secret turns away anger."

BLACK AND BLUE DO-GOODERS

Caring about justice and righteousness between Jews and among all the people of the world is part of our heritage as Jews and Reform Jews. It's a high standard to live up to. Sometimes it's dangerous, as Rabbi David Einhorn discovered in 1861 when he spoke out strongly against slavery in Baltimore before the Civil War. Another believer in righteousness was Stephen Wise who, as a young rabbi, helped underpaid, overworked bakery workers win a ses in 1908. And, during the Great Depression of the 1930s, when hungry people stood on line for handouts of soup and bread, Reform rabbis angered some of their congregants by demanding laws that would require jobs and fair pay for all. Other Reform rabbis and lay people were beaten up and jailed when they rode South in the 1960s to help in the struggle for equal rights for blacks. And many were arrested during demonstrations against the war in Vietnam.

"Single reeds can be broken, but nobody can break many reeds tied together in one bundle," said our rabbis. To tie themselves into a strong bundle, Reform Jews formed a social action committee in 1940. The com-

The person who does not make a choice makes a choice.
Yiddish saying

mittee helped synagogues fight for separation of church and state. They argued, for example, against Christmas trees and Bible readings in the public schools. They also fought against discrimination for reasons of race or sex. In 1972, Reform Jews put their principles to work by graduating the first female Reform rabbi. More female rabbis as well as cantors followed. By 1990 half of the students at Hebrew Union College were women.

YAEL ROMER, BORN 1965

When Yael Romer announced that she was going to study for the rabbinate her mother said, "Why do you have to be a rabbi? Why not a lawyer?" Yael's father said, "Why shouldn't she be a rabbi? I'm proud of her!"

Yael found the same mixed reactions when she graduated from Hebrew Union College and began to work as a congregational rabbi. Her first congregation in Canada accepted her completely. But some members of her second congregation in New Jersey saw her as a nice young woman rather than a spiritual leader. They thought of a rabbi as a man who would answer questions, quote Jewish law, and tell them how to live. Yael sees her work differently. She does not say, "That is wrong–this is what you must do." She says, "Let's study together and find answers."

"I love being a rabbi," says Yael. "It's a great challenge to combine my work as a rabbi with the daily traditions of Jewish life. It makes Judaism come alive for me."

How do kids accept a woman rabbi? Yael said that little kids accept her fully. She tells this story: "A little boy in the congregation would come up to say *Shabbat shalom*, rabbi, after each Friday evening service. One Friday he and his family went to a service at another synagogue that had a male rabbi. At the end of the service the boy's mother said, 'Why don't you say *Shabbat shalom* to the rabbi?' 'There's no rabbi up there, Mommy,' he said. 'Rabbis are women!'"

Rabbi Yael leads morning prayer at the ruins of an 1,800-year-old synagogue in Israel.

A national Religious Action Center (RAC) was set up in Washington, D.C., in 1960. It presents Reform Jewish views to Congress on subjects like support for Israel and abortion rights. Rabbinic students, NFTY leaders, and others come to the RAC to learn how to carry out social action in their own communities and how to communicate with government leaders.

IN OUR OWN BACKYARD

What's happening in our own Jewish backyard? Are there committees to provide bridal gowns for poor brides or to visit the sick as there were in the ghettos of Europe? There may not be a bridal gown committee, but there are many other committees. Jews form committees to raise money for community funds to help the poor and to build day-care centers, retirement homes, and religious schools. Many Jews sit by the phone asking other Jews to contribute to the United Jewish Appeal, which helps Jews in Israel and all over the world. Today the gates of the former Soviet Union have opened and hundreds of thousands of Russian Jews are coming to Israel. Contributions of money are helping to build new homes and make jobs for the immigrants. Settlements and schools of the Reform movement in Israel are helped by grants from the Association of Reform Zionists of America (ARZA). Our own Jewish backyard is as busy as ever with committees.

Good things are being done by kids, too. From Great Neck, New York, to Seattle, Washington, members of NFTY act out their Judaism. A favorite NFTY song says: *Ani ve'atah nishaneh et ha'olam,* "You and I will change the world." In a hundred ways they are working to change at least a little piece of the world. Kids from NFTY's Mitzvah Corps visit, chat, and play checkers with homebound senior citizens. They lead games at day camps for the handicapped, and they hammer and saw and paint at urban renewal projects. In Project Mazon NFTY kids raise money to feed hungry people in the United States and abroad.

BEING GOOD

As Jews we have responsibility for one another in the Jewish community and responsibility to work for justice in the world. There's another kind of responsibility the Torah talks about: responsibility for ourselves. Each of us may do things that nobody else will ever know about. For example, someone can peek at a classmate's paper during a test, steal a pen or a candy bar from a store, or tell an exaggerated story about someone to someone else. These are private acts that nobody else will know about or judge. Does that make them okay? Are we honest, fair, or kind so that we look good to others—or do we also have to look good to ourselves? Think about it and then check your answer with the words of the Torah, Deuteronomy 4:11-20.

A SIMPLE MITZVAH

Let's get back to social responsibility. It may be important, but why is it Jewish? What is especially Jewish about demonstrating for civil rights or painting a slum apartment? Why do we call that kind of act a *mitzvah*? A *mitzvah* is God's command. It tells us how to behave toward one another and toward God. According to ancient rabbinic tradition, the Torah lists 613 *mitzvot*. But a great Jewish leader, Hillel, gave us a simpler way to understand what God wants from us. When someone challenged him to teach the whole Torah while standing on one foot, Hillel answered patiently: "What is hateful to you, do not do to your neighbor. That is the entire Torah. The rest is commentary. Go and study it."

As Reform Jews, we are responsible to go and study and learn more of Torah and *mitzvot*. At the same time we try to live according to Hillel's words: "What is hateful to you, do not do to your neighbor." If you do not want to be alone when you're old and helpless, don't leave others alone. If you do not want to live in a rat-infested slum, try to prevent someone else from being trapped there.

Civil rights, urban renewal, checker games with senior citizens—they're all *mitzvot*. Doing them brings us closer to God and Judaism.

> Judaism is not something we have. It's something we do.
> Sheldon Blank

A LESSON IN TZEDAKAH

In the ghettos, rich Jews were expected to help poor Jews, whether they liked it or not. The writer Sholem Aleichem describes the time little Rabbi Yossifel of Kasrielevky taught a lesson in *tzedakah* to Reb Poliakov, a rich, big-city contractor.

When Reb Poliakov came to the little town of Kasrielevky, he knew he would be bothered by fund-raisers. So he hired a man to turn "beggars" away from the door of his room at the inn. The watchman was gone for a moment—just the moment that Rabbi Yossifel and two of the town's leading citizens arrived. They knocked, entered, and found the great man at his table.

"Who let you in?" roared Poliakov. "Get out!"

The two leading citizens turned and ran. Frail, little Rabbi Yossifel stood his ground. "Reb Poliakov," he began in a shaky voice, "I came to ask you for money to build an Old People's Home in Kasrielevky. . . ."

"Out!" bellowed Poliakov. His face was turning purple with anger.

"...We have m-many poor old p-people in Kasrielevky, they should live and b-be well...." Rabbi Yossifel stuttered on bravely, as Poliakov stood up and raised a heavy hand. "...they have no roof over their heads and m-must..."

Whack! The enraged contractor slapped the little rabbi across the cheek. The rabbi's *kipah* flew off his head.

Yossifel bent to pick up his *kipah*, put it back on his head, and straightened to his full, meagre height. "That slap," he said, "was for me. Now what will you give for the old people of Kasrielevky?"

When Rabbi Yossifel came out of the inn, everyone noticed that one of his cheeks was very, very red. But he had the promise of Poliakov the contractor that an Old People's Home would be built in Kasrielevky.

Adapted from a story by Sholem Aleichem

Some Good Things to Read

Fine, Helen. *At Camp Kee Tov: Ethics for Jewish Juniors*. New York: UAHC, 1961.

Keeping Posted. "Amazing Kids." Vol. XXXIV, No. 1, October 1988. New York: UAHC.

_____."Why Be Good?" Vol. XXXIV, No. 2, November 1988. New York: UAHC.

Vorspan, Albert. *To Do Justly: A Junior Casebook for Social Action*. New York: UAHC, 1983.

Zwerin, Raymond A. *For One Another: Jewish Organizations That Help Us All*. New York: UAHC, 1975.

Activity

WHAT DO *YOU* THINK?

After the murder of six million Jews in the Holocaust, some Jews said:

"The world is an evil place. We can't improve it. We should only worry about strengthening and protecting our own Jewish people."

Does that make sense to you? _____

Why? _____

Why not? _____

During the struggle for civil rights, Jews who lived in the South faced synagogue burnings and threats because Northern Jews were among the leaders of the Civil Rights movement. And during the Vietnam War Jews were called unpatriotic because many of them protested the war.

Was it right for Reform Judaism to take public stands on these matters? _____

What should come first? Write numbers 1, 2, or 3 in the following boxes. Then explain your answer.

☐ social and religious principles and ideals

☐ personal safety

☐ safety of Jews as a group

_____

_____

CELEBRATE JEWISH HOLIDAYS

8

Jewish holidays are specially sweet days that make all the rest of the year taste better—like raisins in a challah or chocolate chips in a cookie. And they are scattered neatly throughout the year. There's always a holiday coming soon. Celebrating a holiday isn't only a pleasure; it's also a *mitzvah*, a commandment. So remember, when you're gobbling matzah balls or clowning around as Haman in a Purim costume, you're also doing a *mitzvah*. You are sharing an experience with Jews all over the world and with other Jews throughout history.

There's another kind of sharing that is part of each Jewish holiday. It is called *tzedakah*, righteousness or charity. We share by giving gifts or money to needy people and by inviting guests for the holiday.

THE HEBREW CALENDAR

The dates of Jewish holidays are reckoned on the Hebrew calendar. It's different from the general calendar because it is based on the moon. There are twelve months in the Hebrew year. Each month begins with the new moon and lasts twenty-nine or thirty days. But that adds up to only 354 days while the earth takes 365 days to travel around the sun. It's important to stay in time with the sun because the seasons are created by the earth's trip around the sun. To keep Jewish holidays from slipping into the wrong season (Chanukah in July or Pesach in January!) every few years our ancestors added an extra month called *Adar Bet*.

We count the years of the Hebrew calendar from the biblical year of creation. To find the Hebrew year, add 3,760 to the general year between January 1 and Rosh Hashanah. Add 3,761 between Rosh Hashanah and January 1.

Season	Holiday	Hebrew Month	Approximate European Month
	Rosh Hashanah Yom Kippur Sukot Simchat Torah	Tishri 1 Tishri 10 Tishri 15-22 Tishri 22	September September-October October October
	Chanukah Tu Bishvat Purim	Kislev 25-Tevet 2 Shevat 15 Adar 14	December January-February February-March

Season	Holiday	Hebrew Month	Approximate European Month
	Pesach (Passover)	Nisan 15-21	April
	Yom Hashoah (Holocaust Remembrance Day)	Nisan 27	April
	Yom Ha'atzmaut (Israel Independence Day)	Iyar 5	April
	Lag Ba'omer	Iyar 18	April-May
	Shavuot	Sivan 6	May-June
	Tishah Be'av	Av 9	July

All Jewish holidays begin at sundown on the eve of the holiday.
Shabbat is the seventh day of each week–all year round.

SHABBAT–THE SEVENTH DAY OF EACH WEEK

The best holiday of all comes once each week. It is Shabbat. And there's a rush to prepare for her. Why for *her*? Because, in Jewish tradition, Shabbat is a lady, a queen. Before the queen arrives, we race around cleaning the house till it shines, polishing the candlesticks, baking or buying a challah, and cooking a delicious Friday night supper with a great dessert. When everything is ready late on Friday afternoon, the family gathers around the table. As the sun sets, we light and bless the Shabbat candles. Then we say a blessing over the wine and the braided bread, challah, and take a deep, peaceful breath. The Shabbat queen brings us a whole day of peace and joy. It's a day when kids can forget math tests and history reports, and adults try not to think about business, jobs, shopping, and bills.

This idea of a day of rest is Judaism's gift to the world. It was given at a time when rich people could lie around every day, all day, while poor people, slaves, and work animals labored all seven days of the week. But the Torah said: "Remember the Shabbat and keep it holy . . . on Shabbat you shall not do any work, neither you nor your son or daughter or servant or ox or donkey nor a stranger who lives with you. . . ." It's a gift we can be proud of.

Some families sing and read aloud at the Shabbat table. Some finish dinner and go to the temple. Most Reform services are on Friday night, *erev* Shabbat. During the service the congregation sings a song called *Lecha Dodi* to welcome the Shabbat queen. The next day is a good time to lie on the grass and smell the flowers, walk, read, or play Scrabble. And then, too soon, the sun is sinking and it's time for the queen to leave.

Shabbat afternoons used to be a not-so-peaceful time for little boys in Eastern Europe. After their fathers had taken an afternoon nap, they would call in their sons and test them on what they had learned in *cheder*, religious school, that week.

We say goodbye to the Shabbat queen by lighting a fat, braided candle with two or more wicks, a *Havdalah* candle. Then we pass a spice box around, say a blessing over the wine, and sip. The flickering candle, the wine, and the nose-tickling spices separate the peaceful Shabbat day from the workaday week.

"Now go and do your homework!" say your parents. Shabbat is over for sure.

ROSH HASHANAH—TISHRI 1

Rosh Hashanah, the Jewish new year, is a thought-filled time. Prayers called *Selichot*, forgiveness, are said before the Rosh Hashanah holiday and during the following Days of Repentance until Yom Kippur. And we think: Have we been loyal friends? Have we held onto grudges? Have we squabbled with our brothers or sisters? Are we taking care of school work, chores, religious school, the cat, the dog, the goldfish? So much to think about! This is also a time to go to your friends, neighbors, or classmates and say, "If I hurt your feelings somehow, please forgive me."

For days before the holiday the mailman brings Rosh Hashanah greeting cards. If you are making cards for your friends, be sure to write on them, *Leshanah tovah tikatevu*, "May you be written down for a good year." According to Jewish tradition, the gates of heaven open at holiday time to allow our prayers to enter, and the great Book of Life is opened so that our names can be written in for the coming year.

Many Reform congregations observe one day of Rosh Hashanah rather than the two days observed by traditional congregations. The temple is full of people. And we know that Jews all over the world are standing in their synagogues, reaching out to one another, and reaching up to God with their prayers. It's a good feeling. Later, at home, we'll dip apple slices in honey and eat round, sweet challah to start the new year with sweetness.

YOM KIPPUR—TISHRI 10

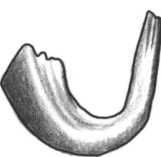

On the eve of Yom Kippur most Jews have an early dinner. Afterwards they light candles, wash the dishes, and hurry to the temple in time for *Kol Nidre*, the first prayer of the holiday. The next morning there won't be mouth-watering whiffs of french toast or pancakes from the kitchen. For many adults and teenagers Yom Kippur is a day of fasting. The temple is quieter on Yom Kippur morning and the prayers are longer than usual. It even looks different. The cantor, the rabbi, and many people in the congregation are wearing white clothing. It's as though we're saying to God: "We're as clean as we can make ourselves. We tried to scrub out the junk, the anger, and the mean behavior. We're listening to You—please listen to us." One of the prayers we recite is *Avinu Malkenu*. It says, "Hear our prayer, open the gates of heaven to our plea, give us strength, and have compassion for us."

Yom Kippur, like Rosh Hashanah, is a time for thinking about the year ahead and reviewing the year that is ending. According to Jewish tradition, our fate will be decided when the Book of Life and the gates of heaven close at sundown.

The temple grows darker as the tired congregation stands for the last prayers. Then, with a final, strong blast of the *shofar*, Yom Kippur ends. *Gemar chatimah tovah*, "May the writing [in the Book of Life] end well," we say to one another and start for home to break the fast.

SUKOT–TISHRI 15-22

Autumn leaves crunch under the table, the decorations of hanging fruits and paper chains bob in the breeze, and a bug drops into the soup from the crisscrossed branches that are the roof of the *sukah*, a booth or shelter. It's a *mitzvah*, a commandment, to eat in the *sukah* during the harvest holiday of Sukot. And it's fun–except for the bug.

Why build a *sukah*? It's to remind us of the shelters that the Jews had lived in during their forty years of wandering in the desert after leaving Egypt. Later, when they became farmers in Israel, the Jews lived in temporary shelters during the harvest period. At holiday time they would load their donkeys or oxen with the best grapes, olives, and other products of the harvest and bring them to the Temple in Jerusalem as a "Thank-You" gift to God.

The trip to the Temple is called a pilgrimage. The Bible also calls for pilgrimages on the holidays of Passover and Shavuot. When we celebrate these holidays, we remember our connection to the golden city of Jerusalem, as well as to the wandering ex-slaves and the farmers of ancient Israel.

Some families begin to build a *sukah* on a porch or in the backyard as soon as Yom Kippur ends. But most of us enjoy the big community *sukah* at the temple. Inside the temple there is a green harvest smell because people bring an *etrog* (a fruit like a lemon) and a *lulav* (a tall palm branch tied to myrtle and willow branches) to wave and carry in a parade during the services.

Ultra-Orthodox boys build a *sukah* in New York City.

Ed Toben

SIMCHAT TORAH—TISHRI 22

Every Shabbat morning throughout the year the Torah scroll is taken out of the *aron* in most congregations and carried around. Then it is unrolled and read, one section or *parashah* each week. At Simchat Torah we reach the last section in which Moses has finished his work of leading the Hebrews through the Sinai Desert. He says goodbye to the people and goes off to die. Then, immediately, we roll the scroll back to the beginning and start the story of creation—"When God began to create the heaven and the earth. . . ." This is a joyful holiday when even young children are called up to say the blessing over the Torah. There is usually a singing, dancing parade as all the Torahs are carried around and around the temple. Every adult can have the honor of carrying the Torah, and every child can join the Torah parade singing and waving a Simchat Torah flag. Big and little, we celebrate our Torah, which has no beginning and no end. We can read it and learn from it all year round, year after year, generation after generation.

CHANUKAH—KISLEV 25 TO TEVET 2

When the days are shortest and darkest, just when you think winter will never end, the bright, happy holiday of Chanukah arrives. For eight days we light candles in the *chanukiyah*, the Chanukah menorah, to celebrate a great victory. It happened about 2,000 years ago when the Syrian empire ruled over Israel. The Syrians demanded that the Jews forget their own religion and worship Syrian gods. Some Jews agreed but others rebelled. They followed Mattathias and his sons up into the mountains and from their hideouts attacked the enemy again and again. The Syrians fought hard. They brought in more fighters and even war elephants, but they were finally driven out of Israel. According to tradition, the Jews then purified the Temple in Jerusalem and prepared to light the great candelabra. Suddenly the found they had enough pure oil to last only one day. They lit it and prayed hard. And, wonder of wonders, the oil burned for eight days!

   Chanukah is a time for inviting friends and family, for giving gifts, lighting candles, playing dreidel, and eating golden potato pancakes and donuts, foods made with oil to remember the miracle of the oil.

TU BISHVAT—SHEVAT 15

Did you have to shovel snow off the driveway this morning? Are you bundled up in a down jacket and earmuffs? No matter. In Israel the almond trees are covered with white blossoms and it's time to plant trees. Jews in every land celebrate Tu Bishvat, the new year of the trees. In many religious schools there will be bowls of dried fruits like those that grow in Israel: raisins, figs, almonds, and carob, a long, brown fruit. Watch your braces on that one! Over the centuries trees were chopped down in Israel leaving bare, eroded hillsides. On Tu Bishvat many families contribute money to the Jewish National Fund to plant trees and help reforest the land. Someplace in Israel there may be a tree with your name on it!

The wise people who wrote the Talmud knew that trees were important. They said: "If you are planting a tree and someone comes to tell you that the Messiah has come . . . finish planting the tree first, then go and greet the Messiah.

At Purim time in Eastern Europe youngsters would dress up, go knocking on doors, and sing: Today is Purim, tomorrow no more. Give me some pennies and throw me out the door.

Hadassah was Esther's Hebrew name. Hadassah, the women's Zionist organization, is named after her.

PURIM—ADAR 14

Purim is the story of a brave, beautiful Jewish woman called Esther and her devout Uncle Mordecai. These two saved their people from being killed by a cruel anti-Jewish villain called Haman. In traditional synagogues, when the Scroll or *Megillah* of Esther was read, the congregation stamped, hissed, and twirled noisemakers when Haman's name was mentioned. Much too noisy, thought early Reform Jews. They tried to keep the reading dignified. But this happy, noisy holiday couldn't be squelched. Today brave Esther, devout Mordecai, stupid King Ahasuerus, and evil Haman are the stars of costume parties and Purim parades in many temples. If a fat hamantash (a triangle-shaped pastry) or a bearded Moses walks into the social hall, watch out—it may be the rabbi. People give *tzedakah* contributions at Purim, feast, and act silly.

PESACH (PASSOVER)—NISAN 15-21

You've borrowed chairs from all the neighbors. The table is stretched as far as it will go. Wine, matzah, a seder dish, and *haggadahs*, or seder books, are all ready. Cousins, aunts, uncles, grandparents, and other guests are in place. It's time to start the Pesach, Passover, seder.

Long before the destruction of the Temple in Jerusalem, Jews were sitting together to retell the story of how they had been freed from slavery in Egypt. But it is more than a story of long-ago. It reminds us to feel as though we ourselves have been brought out of slavery. There's a lot of talking and singing at the seder. *Chad Gadya*, one only kid, is a favorite song. As we sing together, hunt for the *afikoman*, and enjoy the good food, we also remember the important meaning of Pesach: freedom is precious and we need to help our fellow Jews and other people to be free.

No Jew should eat alone on Pesach. We bring home students who are far from home or people without families to share the seder. And many temples make community seders. Along with the real people there's an invisible guest at the seder. The prophet Elijah is said to hurry from home to home, taking a sip from Elijah's cup at each table.

YOM HASHOAH (HOLOCAUST REMEMBRANCE DAY)—NISAN 27

Pesach has passed. The lawn is turning green, daffodils are pushing up, and some days you can run outside without a jacket. At this good time of the year, Jews who were fighting against the Nazis in 1942 in World War Two lost a hopeless battle. Their stronghold in the Warsaw ghetto was destroyed. Most of them were killed. Altogether six million Jews were killed during the Holocaust of World War Two—one out of every three Jews in the world. Most of us lost a grandparent, great-uncle, great-aunt, or distant cousins. The Holocaust is a terrible event to remember in the sweet springtime, but it would be much more terrible if we forgot. We say the *Yizkor* prayer at the temple on Yom Hashoah in memory of the Six Million.

YOM HA'ATZMAUT (ISRAEL INDEPENDENCE DAY)— IYAR 5

Make a big birthday cake for the old-new State of Israel. Three thousand years ago it was an independent country with its own king, army, and capital city of Jerusalem. But don't put three thousand candles on the cake! After Israel was conquered and its people scattered in 70 C.E., Jews still kept coming back to pray at the Western Wall of the destroyed Temple and at other holy sites. Then Jews began to return to Israel (then called Palestine) to build homes and farms. These settlers called themselves Zionists because they were returning to Zion. Finally, in 1948, the new State of Israel was founded, and many more Jews returned to their old-new land from all over the world.

American Jews celebrate Yom Ha'atzmaut with birthday parties, speeches, and rallies. Some cities have Israel Day parades.

Now let's get back to the birthday cake. Counting from 1948, how many candles will you need?

LAG BA'OMER—IYAR 18

Here's a holiday especially for school kids and teachers. It reminds us of two great rabbis and teachers who lived about 1,900 years ago. One was Rabbi Akiva, who supported the war to drive the Romans out of Israel. The other was Shimon bar Yochai, who risked his life to teach Torah to children even though the Romans forbade it. The children would steal off to bar Yochai's hideout carrying bows and arrows. If Roman soldiers caught them, they would say they were going hunting.

Lag Ba'omer comes between Pesach and Shavuot. Close your books, pack the suntan lotion, the frisbee, and sandwiches, and go on a picnic. Fortunately, you will not need to bring a bow and arrows.

SHAVUOT—SIVAN 6

Shavuot is the best-smelling holiday of the Jewish year. We decorate the temple and our homes with bunches of lilacs, roses, and other spring flowers to celebrate the earliest spring harvest in the Land of Israel. It is *Chag Habikkurim*, the holiday of the first fruits, a pilgrimage holiday when Jews once brought gifts of harvest to the Temple in Jerusalem. It is also the holiday of the giving of the Torah. It was at Shavuot, seven weeks after Pesach, that, according to the tradition, the Jews fasted and waited in the Sinai Desert. Finally, Moses came down the slopes of Mount Sinai carrying God's gift of the Ten Commandments for the Jewish people. The Midrash tells us that after that long, tense wait the people were too tired to prepare a cooked meal. They went back to their tents and huts and filled up on cheese and pita. Lucky us—that's why we eat blintzes, knishes, cheese cakes, and other dairy foods at Shavuot. Another good thing about Shavuot is that it's confirmation time. (For more about confirmation, see Chapter 9.)

THE STORY OF RUTH

Ruth was a young, non-Jewish woman who lived in the land of Moab. We read her story from the Bible at Shavuot. Here it is, in a nut shell:

When Ruth's Jewish husband died in Moab, her mother-in-law, Naomi, decided to return to the Land of Israel. Ruth loved Naomi and refused to let her go back alone. "Wherever you go I will go . . . your people will be my people and your God my God," she said. They came to Israel at the time of the spring grain harvest. As a poor stranger in a new land, Ruth had to go out to gather leftover grain for food. She met Boaz, the owner of the field. They fell in love, married, and soon Naomi became a happy grandmother. She would have been even happier if she knew that her grandson Obed, the son of Ruth and Boaz, would be the grandfather of David, the second king of Israel.

TISHAH BE'AV—AV 9

In the middle of the lazy season of swimming, sunbathing, eating ice cream, and reading comes a quiet, solemn day of remembering. Tishah Be'av is a fast day, when many Jews read the Book of Lamentations, the sad words that the prophet Jeremiah wrote after the First Temple was destroyed. We remember also such tragic events from Jewish history as the expulsion of the Jews from Spain in 1492 and the destruction of the Second Temple in 70 C.E. But, even on this sad day, Jews look to a better time. A legend tells that the Messiah, who will come to bring peace and justice to the world, will be born on Tishah Be'av.

Activities

CONNECT THE DOTS IN HEBREW

Connect the letters of the Hebrew *Alef-Bet* to identify each holiday object. If you don't know the order of the letters yet–here they are, going from right to left:

⇐ א, ב, ג, ד, ה, ו, ז, ח, ט, י, כ, ל, מ, נ, ס, ע, פ, צ, ק, ר, ש, ת

Fill in the blanks under each box to name the object and its holiday.

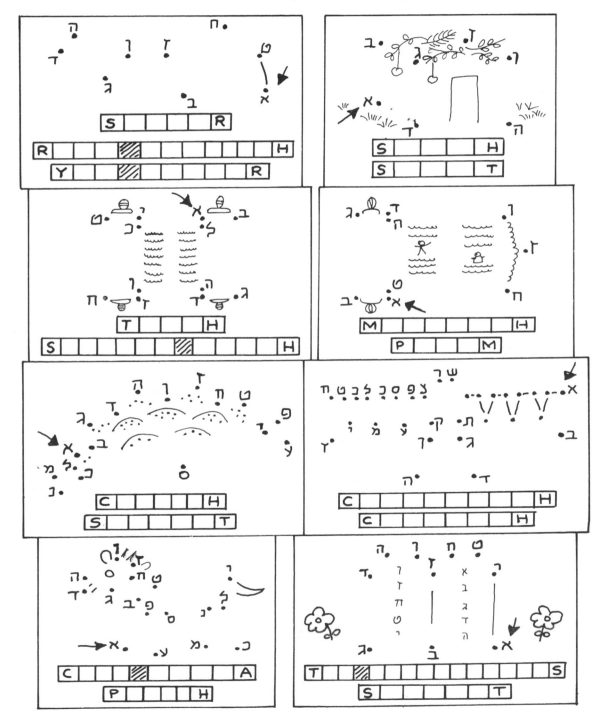

WHAT DO *YOU* THINK?

A Jewish leader called Ahad Ha-Am said: "More than Israel has kept Shabbat, Shabbat has kept Israel."

What did he mean? _____

Do you agree or disagree? _____ Why? _____

DO A SURVEY OF YOUR CLASSMATES

How many kids are there in your class? _____

How many of their families . . .

    light Shabbat candles? _____

    light Chanukah candles? _____

    eat matzah at Passover? _____

    have a Passover seder? _____

    come to services on Shabbat? _____

    come to services on Rosh Hashanah and Yom Kippur? _____

How many of these activities do you and your family do? _____

Is that enough for you? _____

Would you like more? _____ Less? _____

SOME GOOD BOOKS

Burstein, Chaya M. *A First Jewish Holiday Cookbook*. New York: Bonim Books, 1979.

_____.*The Jewish Kids Catalog*. Philadelphia: Jewish Publication Society, 1984.

Chaikin, Miriam. *Sound the Shofar: The Story and Meaning of Rosh Hashanah and Yom Kippur*. New York: Clarion, 1986.

_____.*Make Noise, Make Merry: The Story of Purim*. New York: Clarion, 1986.

Cohen, Barbara. *First Fast*. New York: UAHC, 1987.

Gamoran, Mamie C. *Fun Ways to Holidays*. New York: UAHC, 1951.

Gersh, Harry. *When a Jew Celebrates*. New York: Behrman, 1971.

BAR/BAT MITZVAH, CONFIRMATION, AND OTHER TURNING POINTS

Turning points in our lives are also marked by religious ceremonies. It is as if God and the whole Jewish community are sharing that time with us–whether it's a happy time like a *brit milah* (circumcision) or a sad time like a death.

BAR AND BAT MITZVAH

One of the happy turning points in Jewish life is the celebration of a child becoming a bar or bat mitzvah. The words mean son (*bar*) or daughter (*bat*) of the commandment. At age thirteen, when boys and girls become bar/bat mitzvah, they take on personal responsibility for their part in the religious life of the community. For the first time, the boy or girl is called up to stand before the great parchment scroll–the Torah–God's gift to the Jewish people. The bar/bat mitzvah says the blessings before and after the Torah reading and may also read the last section of the Torah. But the part that makes parents and grandparents burst with pride is the youngster's reading from the Prophets, the *haftarah*. It's an honor that belongs to the bar/bat mitzvah alone.

After this day, the young person will be accepted as a member of a *minyan*, the ten Jews required for a prayer service. In an Orthodox synagogue the bar mitzvah boy will begin to lay *tefilin* (he will wrap a strap holding phylactery boxes around his arm and forehead) for weekday services.

Does that mean it's all over? Have you finished your Jewish education? No. It's a beginning. You're starting to learn about your life and responsibilities as a Jew. And you already took a giant step by learning to read Hebrew so you can participate in prayers and read your *haftarah*. There's a great treasure of Torah, *mitzvot*, traditions, and history yet to come.

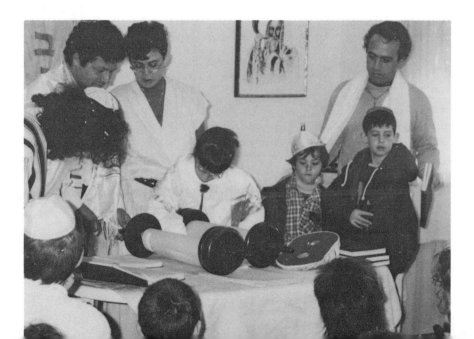

Lilach Adam, a bat mitzvah, reads the Torah on Har Halutz, a Reform settlement in Israel.

Most bar/bat mitzvah kids start off with a blast—a party with lots of guests, gifts, fancy clothing, and good food. And some celebrations add *mitzvot*, commandments and good deeds, to the fun. For example, instead of bringing presents, one bar mitzvah asked his guests to contribute to an organization that helps Ethiopian Jews. Those contributions brought a young Ethiopian boy to Israel. The boys write to each other, and maybe they'll meet one day. A bat mitzvah linked herself to Jewish history by telling her guests about a thirteen-year-old girl who died in the Holocaust. She will never forget the name of the young girl who shared her bat mitzvah.

CONFIRMATION

Early Reform Jews didn't see any sense in becoming bar mitzvah. They thought that preparing a child to read from the Torah didn't teach him the principles and duties of his religion. Reform Jews chose a different turning-point celebration—a confirmation. This was like a school graduation that celebrated the end of a period of study. Before the ceremony, boys and girls took an exam on everything they had learned in Jewish religious school. The confirmation ceremony was a thoughtful, serious time when the boys and girls expressed their feeling of commitment to Judaism. After some years, the confirmation ceremony began to take place in ninth and tenth grades instead of earlier. The whole class would be confirmed in the synagogue during Shavuot. This flower-filled holiday that celebrates the giving of the Torah to the Jewish people is a perfect time for young Jews to confirm their belief in Judaism.

Today Reform Judaism gives us two happy turning points. There's a bar/bat mitzvah at age thirteen and, after more study, a confirmation at age fifteen or sixteen.

MARRIAGE

When a soul comes down from heaven, it contains both male and female elements. The male elements enter a baby boy; the female elements enter a baby girl. And, if they are worthy, God will bring them together again in marriage someday.

From the *Zohar*, a mystical holy book

Marriage is a turning point that two people reach, but coming from different directions. Then they turn together and walk on along the same path. Kids used to sing a teasing song about marriage. Maybe you sang it, too. Remember? "First comes love, then comes marriage, then comes baby in a baby carriage!" In Jewish life the song makes sense. At the *brit* ceremony of a baby boy people say, "May he grow up to Torah, to marriage, and to good deeds." And, when the baby grows up and gets married, the parents of the bride and groom and all the guests happily repeat the Torah's words, "Be fruitful and multiply." Judaism stresses love, marriage, and a baby carriage—just as the song does.

A Jewish wedding ceremony usually takes place in a temple, under a *chupah*, a square wedding canopy held up on poles by friends or family members. The *chupah* represents the home that the new couple will share. As they stand under the *chupah*, the rabbi or the bride and groom read their wedding agreement aloud before the guests and witnesses. The agreement is called a *ketubah*. The traditional *ketubah* is written in Aramaic, an ancient Middle Eastern language. It contains guarantees from the groom to provide and care for his wife and even lists the amount of money he will pay her if they are divorced. A modern *ketubah* may be written by

A *ketubah* is often decorated with colorful animals and flowers. This *ketubah* by Jeffrey Allon in Jerusalem has peacocks, fish, and bright, rising suns.

both the bride and groom, in Hebrew and English. It may tell of the promises and the goals that the new partners share. After the ceremony, comes the eating, singing, and dancing as everybody celebrates. Hurray, a new family has joined the people of Israel!

Marriage between a Jew and a non-Jew is called an intermarriage. Since a marriage performed by a rabbi is a Jewish religious ceremony, many rabbis will not perform a marriage between people of different religions. Some rabbis do perform intermarriages. Couples who intermarry and their children are welcome in Reform temples.

DIVORCE

Sometimes marriages get into trouble. If the husband and wife bring their problems to a rabbi, the rabbi will try to help them work out their disagreements. Ending a marriage by divorce is the last resort—when no agreement can be reached. In Reform Jewish tradition only a civil (non-religious) divorce is necessary. But Conservative, Orthodox, and some Reform Jews want a religious divorce called a *get*. The *get* is a short statement that a man is divorcing his wife. It is written by a scribe before a court of three rabbis and two witnesses. After the rabbis make sure that the wife agrees to the *get*, the husband hands the *get* to her. She accepts it, he leaves, and then she leaves.

JEWS-BY-CHOICE

There have been many Jews-by-choice in the course of Jewish history. (See the story of Ruth in Chapter 8.) But the steps toward becoming a Jew are not easy. When a non-Jew comes to a rabbi and says, "I want to become a Jew," the rabbi doesn't jump up and down joyfully and say, "Come on in, the water's fine!" Rabbis warn the person that he or she will need to study Jewish religion, history, customs, the Hebrew language, and prayer before being considered for conversion. After thorough preparation, the

The true convert is dearer to God than the Israelites. If the Israelites had not seen the thunder and lightning on Mount Sinai . . . they might not have accepted the holy Torah. But the convert who did not see these things has opened his heart to the Holy One. Who can be dearer to God?

Midrash

At a *brit*,
a friend or
relative is chosen
to hold the baby.
He is called
a *sandak*.

God said to Abraham:
This is My covenant, which you
shall keep, between Me and you
and your seed after you. Every
manchild among you shall be circumcised. And you shall circumcise
the flesh of your foreskin. And it
shall be a sign of the covenant
between Me and you.
                    Genesis 17:10-11

Legends tell that the prophet
Elijah takes a sip of wine at each
seder table. Between seders he
wanders through the world helping needy people. Luckily for baby
boys he also attends every *brit*.
Jews set aside a chair for Elijah at
the *brit*. There's also a chair for
Elijah on the *bimah* of the
synagogue.

Jew-by-choice is ready for the conversion ceremony. Conservative rabbis
normally require that a man be circumcised before conversion and that
both men and women dip themselves in a *mikveh*, a special ritual bath.
Some Reform rabbis ask that a man have a symbolic circumcision with a
drop of blood and that both men and women go to the *mikveh*.

After conversion the Reform Jewish community expects a Jew-by-choice
to belong to a synagogue, observe Jewish customs and holidays, and give
tzedakah. Maybe this doesn't seem fair. After all, some people who are
born Jewish don't follow their own religious traditions and yet they're considered Jewish. We seem to accept the idea of "once a Jew, always a Jew."
It would take a terrible crime against God and the Jewish people to cause
a community to excommunicate (throw out) a member. But, when someone chooses to become a Jew, the community usually welcomes the person
warmly and asks for wholehearted belief and action.

BRIT MILAH AND BRIT CHAYIM

You can't prepare for the number one turning point in your life: your circumcision covenant (for boys) and your covenant of life (for girls). Your
parents carry you across that turning point. A few days after you are born,
they set you on course for a Jewish life.

Circumcision for Jewish male babies has been done for almost 4,000
years. The Bible tells us that circumcision of all Jewish males is a sign of
the covenant or agreement between Abraham and God. To circumcise
means to cut the foreskin off the penis of the baby boy. The cutting is
traditionally done by a *mohel* on the eighth day after the baby's birth.
Today the Reform movement trains doctors, both men and women, to be
ritual circumcisers. The family, friends, and rabbi or *mohel* who attend
the ceremony recite a prayer of hope that the baby will grow up to a life
of study, marriage, and good deeds. The baby is given his Hebrew name
and a few drops of wine. Then, hopefully, he falls asleep, and everyone
else enjoys a festive snack.

A female baby's entrance into the covenant or *brit chayim* is more
peaceful than a boy's. In an Orthodox synagogue the father is honored
with an *aliyah* to the Torah on the first Shabbat after the baby's birth.
He says the blessings before and after the Torah reading, and the baby's
birth and Hebrew name are announced from the *bimah*. After the service
there is a *Kiddush* of wine and cake. In a Reform temple both parents are
honored, usually within a few weeks after the baby's birth. Many families
also celebrate the *brit chayim* in their homes as a naming ceremony. They
prepare special prayers and readings and, of course, good food.

DEATH

Throughout Jewish history there have been different ideas about what
happens after death. The Torah doesn't speak of heaven or hell. In the
Torah death is final. But years later, when the Talmud was being written,
ideas of heaven and hell, of life after death, and of the coming of the
Messiah became important in Jewish life. Today many Jews, including
Reform Jews, have gone back to the Torah's view and see death as a last
turning point. After death a person cannot come back to life. The soul or

spirit returns to God and the person remains alive in our thoughts, in photographs, and in the memories of experiences and feelings we've shared.

Jewish ways of dealing with death help families and friends come through this hard time. When a person dies, he or she is usually buried within twenty-four hours, after a religious funeral service. Traditionally, the parents, children, wife or husband, brothers, and sisters of the dead person spend seven days of mourning in their home. This is called "sitting *shivah*," seven. Some families observe a three-day mourning period. People come to sit with them, to talk and comfort them, to remember and tell old stories, and to laugh and cry together. They bring gifts of sweets, send certificates of trees planted in Israel, or make contributions to charities in honor of the dead person. Each day the Mourner's *Kaddish* prayer is recited by a *minyan* in the home. It is a prayer that praises God and has taken on the added meaning of expressing our love for those who have died and our sadness at losing them.

It is customary for mourners to recite *Kaddish* for thirty days after the death. This period is called *Sheloshim*, thirty. Traditionally, children who have lost a parent recite the *Kaddish* prayer for a full year. In a Reform temple the whole congregation stands and joins in the Mourner's *Kaddish*. It is a time to remember our own dead and to remember those who died in the Holocaust because most left no children to recite *Kaddish* in their names.

As time passes, the pain of sadness and loneliness may ease. But we don't forget the dead. Each year, on the anniversary of the death, Jews light a thick memorial candle called a *yahrzeit* candle or, in Hebrew, a *ner zikaron*. It burns for twenty-four hours.

> If the rich could hire the poor to die for them, the poor would make a very good living.
> Yiddish saying

Activities

TURNING POINTS

Everybody's life has happy times, sad times, and times when the person discovers new ideas and begins to move in a new direction. Those times are turning points.

What turning points have there been in your life? How were they celebrated?

In each box describe an important turning point.

For example:

> I started nursery school when I was 3. I cried and wanted to go home. My parents got me a big, new fire truck.

Simchat Bat or Brit

What's next?

WHAT IS YOUR FIRST JEWISH MEMORY?

A holiday? A food? A story? A song? _____

_____

Bring something to class that reminds you of that time and tell about it.
Draw a picture that describes the memory.

MATCH THESE WORDS TO THEIR MEANINGS

1 *tefilin*	1 circumciser
2 *brit milah*	2 going up (to Israel or to the *bimah*)
3 *brit chayim*	3 seven days of mourning
4 *chupah*	4 daughter of the commandment
5 *aliyah*	5 son of the commandment
6 *haftarah*	6 thirty days of mourning
7 bar mitzvah	7 divorce
8 bat mitzvah	8 phylacteries
9 *get*	9 naming ceremony
10 *mohel*	10 prayer praising God as we remember the dead
11 *shivah*	11 reading from the Prophets
12 *Sheloshim*	12 wedding canopy
13 *Kaddish*	13 circumcision

Some Good Books

Chaikin, Miriam. *Finders Weepers*. New York: Harper Junior Books, 1980.
Efron, Benjamin, and Rubin, Alvan D. *Coming of Age: Your Bar/Bat Mitzvah*. New York: UAHC, 1977.
Schnur, Steven. *The Narrowest Bar Mitzvah*. New York: UAHC, 1986.
_____. *The Return of Morris Schumsky*. New York: UAHC, 1987.
Syme, Daniel B. *The Jewish Home: A Guide for Jewish Living*. New York: UAHC, 1988.
Wolff, Ferida. *Pink Slippers: Bat Mitzvah Blues*. Philadelphia: Jewish Publication Society, 1989.

10 REFORM JEWISH YOUTH GROUPS AND SUMMER PROGRAMS

When you're lying on the grass and staring up at a million stars, it may be easier to think about God than in the religious school classroom.

When you and your friends are pushing and pulling one another up a steep trail, it may be easier to understand about responsibility and friendship than in a classroom.

And, when you're building a model of a kibbutz watchtower or learning to dance the horah, it's easier to learn Hebrew words and learn about Israel than in a classroom.

Prayer, singing Hebrew songs, enjoying Shabbat, and many other Jewish activities feel different and sometimes more meaningful when they are shared with friends at a NFTY (Reform Jewish youth group) meeting or at a UAHC camp.

NFTY AT HOME

NFTY stands for North American Federation of Temple Youth. It is an organization of Reform temple teenagers, founded in 1939. Today there are over 450 NFTY local youth groups with approximately 10,000 members in North America. After 1967 a Reform youth movement was formed in Israel, too. Groups of NFTY (pronounced "nifty") kids meet in temples each week. They have thoughtful, sometimes loud and heated discussions on such subjects as interfaith dating, women's roles in Judaism, gay rights, and separation of church and state. Some NFTY members join the Torah Corps and study together. Others act out their *tzedakah* and social responsibilities through the Mitzvah Corps and Project Mazon. They raise money for food and work to shelter poor and homeless people. With all this, NFTY members still have time for games, parties, dances, and outings.

NFTY's activities give kids a personal tie to their temple. It's not only a place of worship; it's also their place for fun, friends, and living with Judaism. Every few months the ties reach further as NFTY kids from entire regions meet at conclaves or conferences to share ideas, plan activities, and renew friendships.

FUN IS IMPORTANT, TOO
When a person dies and goes to face the Almighty, he will have to account for all the pleasures of life that he failed to enjoy.

Talmud

This serious discussion is taking place at a NFTY weekend conference in Wisconsin.

NFTY AT CAMP

One camper described camp as "a place where you're on your own, with no grown-ups getting on your case." Another camper said, "It's great. Everybody is equal. No one cares about clothes. You're *you*!"

For years individual congregations had been running summer camps for their members. The camps were such a success that, in 1951, the Union bought sites in Oconomowac, Wisconsin, and Saratoga, California, to serve several congregations. Later more sites were bought. Today there are UAHC camps in almost every region of the United States.

Campers live in cabins or tents. They can choose among several different programs. There are arts, crafts, nature study, swimming, and other sports. Older campers add construction, canoeing, rock climbing, backpacking, and more. Hebrew language and Jewish themes are part of every activity. One camper remembers reciting morning prayers on a cross-country hike that took several days. The hikers carefully carried a Torah so they could do the Torah reading on Shabbat. One morning, they stopped for prayer at a gas station. It was a spiritual fill-up.

At the end of each week campers do a thorough cleanup of bunks and campgrounds, dress in white, and gather for Shabbat prayers and songs. The white shorts and shirts gleam in the night and the singing rises up, up, up to the dark sky. The next day has a holiday calmness that carries through the relaxed Shabbat morning prayers, quiet discussions, lazy swimming and sports, and finally the *Havdalah* service, which ends the day of rest.

Camp is a place to live Judaism daily in a natural way. Even the rabbi becomes a natural part of the scene. He or she may lead prayer services in the morning and then spend the afternoon playing shortstop in old, cutoff jeans. Prayer services become personal, too. Campers think about the prayers and often write prayers of their own. And visiting counselors and campers from Israel add Hebrew songs, dances, and language to the camp scene.

TRICKY, TRICKY

During a counselors' meeting at Olin-Sang-Ruby, the UAHC's first camp, the campers lifted the camp director's bed and bureau up to the roof of his cabin. He came back exhausted and fell into . . . the floor.

The girls at camp stole the right shoe of each boy and lined up the shoes on the hillside to spell a word. Which word? They won't say.

One night the counselors came back to their cabins and found the wrong kids. All the groups had switched cabins.

On another busy night somebody or somebodies (still unidentified) pulled the center posts out of each tent. With a "whoosh" the tents collapsed onto the sleepers.

CAMPERS SAY . . .

You get to be like brothers and sisters with your bunkmates–even better. And those friendships go on long after camp ends.

Amy

I always thought being Jewish meant just going to services. At camp we talked about people and their problems. Now I see *tikkun olam*, repairing the world, as part of my Judaism.

Lisa

Did I learn Hebrew at camp! I had to. If I didn't learn how to say "Pass the food" in Hebrew, I would've starved to death!

Mark

NFTY ABROAD

NFTY trips to Europe and Israel help kids to understand their world and their Jewish roots in other lands. The grandparents or great grandparents of many NFTY members grew up across the sea in Europe, Africa, or Asia. One NFTY trip took youngsters to Spain. They saw the graceful synagogues the Jews had built during the golden age of Jewish life in Spain. Then they traced the tragic expulsions and forced conversions of Jews that followed the golden age. Other NFTY groups joined Israeli teenagers to visit Poland and walk through the Nazi death camps. One young American stood for a long time at the edge of a pit at Maidanek where many Jewish victims are buried. "I stood wondering–are my great-uncles buried here," he said quietly.

NFTY groups spend several weeks in Israel. More American youngsters visit Israel through NFTY's Teen Tours than through any other Jewish organization. With Israeli kids they hike and ride buses to explore the deserts, forests, farms, and cities of Israel. They pick apples, study Hebrew, swim, dance, get sunburned, and go tubing on the Jordan River. It's fun–and, along with the fun, campers get a taste of Israel's accomplishments and problems.

"There were twenty-seven of us Americans traveling with eighteen Israelis," said a NFTY member. "We Americans were talking about which college we'd go to next year. But for the Israelis this was the last summer before they went into the army. It made college seem a little trivial."

Youth group, camp, conferences, and trips are live-in learning. NFTY members and campers form friendships, work together, and feel Judaism each day as a happy and important part of their lives. These programs can't replace classroom study, but they can make the book learning come alive and matter more than ever.

Activities

NFTY LOGOS

Most NFTY groups and camps have their own designs or logos for T-shirts and sweatshirts. If your group has a logo, draw it on the shirt below.

You can also make one up. Draw a symbol that tells about your group–Jewish, dancing, scouting, Zionist. . . .

To draw the logo on a shirt, use special textile crayons. You'll find them at art supply or hobby stores.

GREAT NFTY PLACES

To find out about a great NFTY place, copy each numbered drawing into the empty box that has the same number.

11 HEBREW

A TRUE FAIRY TALE

Do you remember the story of Sleeping Beauty, the princess who was placed under a spell by a wicked fairy and slept for a hundred years? Sleeping Beauty was finally awakened by a handsome prince who broke through a thicket to find her. She and her prince married, reigned together over their kingdom, and lived happily ever after.

Jews have a Sleeping Beauty story, too. But it's not about a beautiful, young princess. It's about a beautiful, ancient language: the Hebrew language. Once upon a time the Hebrew language was spoken by all the people of Israel. Farmers, kings, queens, prophets, merchants, and parents scolded, decreed, prayed, prophesied, and peddled in Hebrew. The Torah and later the *Mishnah* were written in Hebrew. As years passed, the wheeler-dealers of Israel who had business with other countries began to use such other languages of the area as Aramaic, Greek, and Latin. The final blow to Hebrew, the spell that put her to sleep, was the exile of the Jewish people from their land.

In foreign lands Jews couldn't use Hebrew. They had to speak the languages that were used around them. But the Jews could not, would not give up as easily as the countrymen of the fairy-tale princess. Hebrew was their link to the Torah, to their land, and to other Jews. They found ways to keep their language half-awake. In prayers and Torah study they used Hebrew. Little boys studied Hebrew as part of their religious education. It became a *leshon hakodesh*, a holy language, for holy purposes. Jews also used the Hebrew alphabet, the *Alef-Bet*, to write the languages that they spoke each day. A Jewish merchant living in Germany six hundred years ago would speak German to his customers all day. Then in the evening he would write his business records in German words but in the Hebrew alphabet. The Jewish language called Yiddish grew out of a combination of old German written in the Hebrew alphabet, with a large number of added Hebrew words. Other Jewish languages like Ladino and Judeo-Arabic were combinations of Spanish or Arabic with Hebrew words—all written in the Hebrew alphabet.

Except for a short awakening during the golden age of Jewish culture in Spain, Princess Hebrew stayed fast asleep for centuries. In daily life Jews couldn't use Hebrew to buy fish in the marketplace, read a novel, or flirt with girlfriends or boyfriends. It wasn't until the late 1700s and early 1800s that a prince or two turned up to try to awaken her. But they were puny princes. They were Jews who left the ghetto and moved into the non-Jewish world. They spoke German and Russian in daily life but wanted to revive Hebrew as a literary language for scholars, poets, and novelists. Not many people were interested. Princess Hebrew may have blinked and yawned, but she didn't bother to wake up.

A few decades later Jews in Europe began to dream of building their own Jewish homeland. They called themselves Zionists. Some of them packed up and moved to Palestine. Then the interest in a working Hebrew language grew strong. And that's when a brave and powerful prince pushed his way through the thicket of centuries, kissed the princess and woke her. The prince was Eliezer Ben-Yehuda, a skinny Russian Jew with a pointy, little beard and pince-nez eyeglasses that squeezed his long nose.

Ben-Yehuda declared that a revived Jewish nation living in its ancient homeland had to speak its own reawakened Hebrew language. He and his family came to Palestine in 1881 and refused to speak anything but Hebrew. Other Zionists followed the lead of the Ben-Yehuda family, speaking only Hebrew and turning the holy language into a hard-working daily language.

Ben-Yehuda formed a language committee to dress up the old-fashioned, sleepy princess. The committee developed new words from ancient Hebrew roots–words for bicycle, train, babysitter, pineapple, washing machine, and more. Then Ben-Yehuda wrote a giant dictionary, which included all the new and old words. Little by little the language of kings and prophets was getting used to the modern world.

The language committee is still hard at work. Now they are wrestling with words like clone, extraterrestrial being, and hard rock. The Ben-Yehuda dictionary has been revised again and again. Princess Hebrew is wide awake now, growing and stretching and ready to live happily ever after, into the twenty-first, twenty-second, and twenty-third centuries . . . at least.

HEBREW IN DOUBLE TIME

Hundreds of thousands of immigrants flooded into Israel after the state was declared in 1948. They spoke Polish, Russian, Arabic, Yemenite, Yiddish, Greek, Dutch, Amharic, Parsi, English, Hindustani, and a few other languages. People had to speak sign language to understand each other. The government started hurry-up, language-learning classes called *ulpanim*. The immigrants quickly learned necessary words and phrases so that they could buy groceries and take buses and trains. The *ulpan* system was so successful that language schools in other countries adopted it. Today Israel's *ulpanim* are filled with new Russian and Ethiopian immigrants.

Can you imagine a popular American song praising Webster's dictionary? This popular Israeli song praises the language-prince and dictionary writer Eliezer Ben-Yehuda.

ELIEZER BEN-YEHUDA
Words by Yaron London and tune by Matti Kaspi

Like the prophets who jealously loved God
He jealously loved the verb, the adjective, and the noun.
And at midnight, with the lamp lit at the window,
He would write piles and piles of pretty words,
Flying words that rolled from the tongue.

Eliezer, when will you go to bed?
You are bent almost double over your desk.
Hebrew has waited 2,000 years;
It will wait for you till dawn.

"If Hebrew rested 2,000 years–so what?
We'll wake her–and we'll invent words,
Words for 'initiative,' an 'iron,' a 'bomb,' and 'furniture.'"
With a feather quill and flowing script
He wrote "cauliflower"; he wrote "ice cream,"
He wrote the whole dictionary of Ben-Yehuda.

His quill never rested as he kept creating words.
And each night the language grew
So that it didn't recognize itself, couldn't recognize itself
With the coming of dawn.

HEBREW IN THE SYNAGOGUE

How much Hebrew should there be in a synagogue service? Since it is important to understand each word of the service, shouldn't Jews pray in their familiar, daily language?

These questions have been discussed since the beginning of the Reform movement. In the early 1800s Reform Rabbi Samuel Levi Eger feared that, if other languages were used in the synagogue, the main purpose of learning Hebrew would disappear. But it would be a terrible loss if people stopped learning Hebrew because the language was a bond between Jews everyplace. Eger said: "If we in Germany pray in German, the Jews of France in French, those in Italy in Italian, the bundle will come apart."

Other Reform Jews disagreed with Eger. They pointed to the *Kaddish* and *Kol Nidre* prayers in the *siddur* that are in the Aramaic language and said, in effect, "If the ancient Jews switched from Hebrew to the local language, so can we." Reform congregations in Germany and the United States began to use only a few lines of Hebrew in their services. The rest of the service was in German or English. And new songs were added to the prayer services in German or English. The Reform movement's Pittsburgh Platform of 1885 described a Judaism that cared a lot about the ideas of God and prayer but much less about Jewish customs and the Hebrew language.

Seventy years before the State of Israel was born an early Zionist named Peretz Smolenskin said: "You ask me what good a dead language [Hebrew] will do for us. I will tell you. It confers honor on us, strengthens us, unites us into one people. . . . We have no country. Only one relic still remains from the ruins of our ancient glory–the Hebrew language."

Long before Reform Judaism began Jewish leaders worried about the fact that many Jews couldn't understand Hebrew prayer. Chasidim (very Orthodox Jews) in Eastern Europe reached out to those with no Hebrew learning and told them that simple, sincere prayers were even more welcome than the prayers of learned Hebrew rabbis. This chasidic story expresses that idea.

THE LEARNED CARPENTER

Rabbi Isaac Luria used to pray to God with all his heart and soul. One day an angel flew by and whispered to him that his poor neighbor, Abraham the carpenter, prayed even more earnestly than he. This Abraham must be a very learned man, thought Rabbi Isaac. I must speak to him. He hurried down the street and found Abraham sawing wood in front of his small house.

"Excuse me for interrupting you," said Rabbi Isaac. "I see you are a carpenter."

"That I am," said Abraham.

"Aha. Are you also a scholar?" asked the rabbi.

"No," Abraham answered sadly. "I don't even know all the letters of the *Alef-Bet*. I know only from *alef* to *yod*.

Rabbi Isaac was puzzled. Could the angel have made a mistake? "If you don't know the *Alef-Bet*, how do you say your prayers?" he asked.

"I just repeat the letters that I know over and over again," said Abraham, "and I ask God to put them together into a prayer."

As the 1900s moved along, Reform Jews began to swing back to more traditional observance. More and more people wanted to feel part of the great sweep of Jewish history and to enjoy Jewish holidays and traditions. Hebrew prayer took a larger share of the service and bar/bat mitzvah celebrations slowly became part of Reform services. Now boys and girls *had* to study Hebrew. How else could they read the Torah and *haftarah*? When the State of Israel was established, with Hebrew as its national language, interest in Hebrew study in religious schools grew even stronger.

HEBREW AND YOU

How does Hebrew study affect you? Is it tough, terrible, or terrific? Here's how some sixth graders answered the question:

Tough

- going to religious school after a full day at regular school
- learning a new alphabet
- writing backwards, from right to left
- figuring out the dots and dashes that are vowels; later learning to read grown-up Hebrew with no vowels at all

Terrific

- being able to follow prayers in temple
- reading Torah in the *original*
- being able to say some words to Jews of other lands; to speak a little Hebrew when you visit Israel
- knowing a language that linked the Jews together for thousands of years

NAMES

During the long centuries when Hebrew was not a daily language, Jews found a simple way to use Hebrew a million times each day. They gave their children Hebrew names:

"Ya'akov, get away from the cookie jar!"
"Rivka, when are you going to get your homework done?"
"Avi, bring a pail of water, please."

Even when a Jew used a name that came from another language, he or she usually had a Hebrew name as well. The Hebrew name is used at specific times throughout a person's life. A Jew is called up to the Torah in the synagogue by his or her Hebrew name. At a *brit*, baby-naming, wedding, funeral, and religious divorce the Hebrew name is used. And, when a non-Jew is converted to Judaism, he or she chooses a Hebrew name.

According to the tradition of most European and Western Jews, babies are named after people who have died. Jews of Eastern backgrounds may use names of living people. In both traditions the names are given because Jews want to remember and honor those who have come earlier. It is very sad when people die without leaving family who can remember them—as happened with many who died in the Holocaust during World War Two. We remember Holocaust victims during the *Yizkor* memorial service in the synagogue.

SPEAK HEBREW

You can talk to another Jew anyplace by using one of these words or phrases.

Phrase	How to Say It*	What It Means	When to Use It
שָׁלוֹם	sha-<u>lom</u>	hello, goodbye, peace	coming and going
בֹּקֶר טוֹב	<u>bo</u>-ker tov	good morning	in the morning
לַיְלָה טוֹב	<u>laye</u>-lah tov	good night	at night
מַה שְׁלוֹמְךָ	mah shelom-<u>cha</u>	how are you	when you meet

Phrase	How to Say It*	What It Means	When to Use It
לְהִתְרָאוֹת	le-hit-ra-ot	be seeing you	when you leave
מַזָּל טוב	ma-zal tov	good luck	at any time
בְּתֵאָבוֹן	be-te-a-von	good appetite	before eating
לְחַיִּים	le-cha-yim	to life (cheers)	before drinking
לַבְּרִיאוּת	lab-ri-ut	bless you!	after a sneeze
חַג שָׂמֵחַ	chag sa-me-ach	happy holiday	at holiday time
שַׁבָּת שָׁלוֹם	sha-bat sha-lom	peaceful Sabbath	on the Sabbath
בְּבַקָשָׁה	be-va-ka-shah	please	at any time
תּוֹדָה	to-dah	thank you	at any time
יוֹם הוּלֶדֶת שָׂמֵחַ	yom hu-le-det sa-me-ach	happy birthday	at birthdays

*Stress the syllable that's underlined. Ch is a sound you make when you're gargling.

In English or Hebrew letters, fill in the suitable Hebrew phrase under each picture.

Activities

HEBREW NAMES

What is your Hebrew name? _____

What does it mean? _____

What are your parents' Hebrew names? _____

Are you named for somebody? _____ If so, who? _____

Ask your parents to tell you about the person whose name you've been given.

Below are lists of Hebrew names and their meanings. Match them by writing the numbers of the meanings next to the names (some names have the same meanings). Check your answers on page 96.

Boys' Names	Girls' Names	Meanings of the Hebrew Names	
Adam ____	Alisa ____	1 palm tree	19 springtime
Alon ____	Aviva ____	2 blossom	20 sympathy
Ami ____	Devora ____	3 rose	21 dove
Ari ____	Dina ____	4 level place	22 bear
Avi (Avraham) ____	Elana ____	5 mountain goat	23 good
Benjamin ____	Naomi ____	6 beauty	24 he will follow
Daniel ____	Nitza ____	7 of the earth	25 oak
David ____	Noa ____	8 God is my judge	26 song
Dov ____	Orli ____	9 beloved	27 my people
Ehud ____	Rina ____	10 the Lord is God	28 father of many
Haim ____	Rivka ____	11 song	or my father
Joel ____	Sharon ____	12 who is like God?	29 activity
Matan ____	Shira ____	13 pretty	30 tree
Michael ____	Shoshana ____	14 happy	31 bee
Noam ____	Tamar ____	15 pleasant	32 son of my right hand
Ron ____	Tova ____	16 lion	33 life
Uri ____	Varda ____	17 justice	34 my light
Ya'akov ____	Yael ____	18 wolf	35 my light
Yona ____	Yaffa ____		36 gift
Zev ____	Yonat ____		

Some Good Books

Burstein, Chaya M. *The Kids Hebrew – English Wordbook*. Philadelphia: Jewish Publication Society, 1992.

Drucker, Malka. *Eliezer Ben-Yehuda: The Father of Modern Hebrew*. New York: Lodestar Books, 1987.

Samuel, Edith. *Your Jewish Lexicon*. New York: UAHC, 1982.

Watson, Carole. *One Thousand First Words*. Israel: Massada Press, 1981.

_____.*Book of My World*. Israel: Massada Press, 1981.

12 THE STATE OF ISRAEL

Better a bad peace than a good war.   Yiddish saying

Whenever a treaty of peace is signed, God is present.
                    Chasidic saying by
                    Nachman of Bratzlav

- It is a little larger than the state of New Jersey, about 8,000 square miles.
- It has a religious-ethnic mishmash of Jews, Muslims, and Christians.
- It is in the middle of the Middle East, about 6,000 miles east of New York and about 8,600 miles east of California.
- It has been at war for all of its existence.
- It is bordered on the west by the Mediterranean Sea, on the east by Jordan and Syria, on the north by Lebanon, and on the south by Egypt.
- The climate is like that of Southern California: warm, dry summers and cool, wettish winters.
- It is a new country, established on May 15, 1948; but it is also a very old country.

How can Israel be old and new at the same time?
Why has Israel been at war for so long?
What's a religious-ethnic mishmash?

Look for the answers to these questions and others in this photo album of Israel.

PHOTO ALBUM

1. **People praying at the Western Wall of the Temple Mount**

   This wall is all that is left of the ancient Holy Temple in Jerusalem. The Romans destroyed it in 70 C.E., almost 2,000 years ago. That meant the end of the Jewish land of Judea-Israel. The Jews fled or were driven into exile. But they couldn't forget their land, God, the Hebrew Bible, or their fellow Jews. Over the centuries Jews kept coming back to the Holy Land to die.

Ed Toben

2. **Children in Kfar Tavor in 1913**

   In the late 1800s many national groups in Europe were struggling for independence. Some Russian Jews said, "It's time for us to rebuild our homeland, too–right now!" They formed a group called Bilu (the initials of the Hebrew words that mean "House of Jacob, let's get going!"), made their way to Palestine, and began to build Kfar Tavor and other villages.

Central Zionist Archives

3. **Theodor Herzl, the founder of modern Zionism**

   Theodor Herzl, a Zionist leader, met with kings and presidents to get support for the establishment of a Jewish state in Palestine. He brought Jews together to form the World Zionist Organization. Herzl's efforts to get international support failed. But after World War One the League of Nations (an early United Nations) gave nation status to six Arab countries and agreed to a Jewish homeland in Palestine under British supervision or mandate.

Central Zionist Archives

4. **Lunchtime in the fields of Tel Yosef in 1922**

   Excited young Zionists came to Palestine to build homes. The Jewish National Fund collected money abroad and bought land from Arab landowners, drained swamps, planted trees, and helped set up villages and kibbutzim, collective farms. Arabs from nearby lands also came to settle in Palestine. Many Arabs feared that Jews would take over the country. They attacked settlements and set fire to fields and young forests. "Stop the Jewish immigration!" they demanded.

Central Zionist Archives

5. The tragedy of Europe's Jews trapped in the Holocaust is portrayed in this sculpture on an Israeli hilltop.

More and more Jews tried to reach Palestine after the Nazis came to power in Germany in 1933. The Nazis had two major goals: to conquer Europe and to destroy the Jews. When Europe's Jews tried to escape, they found the gates of other countries closed against them. Even the gates of Palestine were closed because the British would allow only small numbers to enter. During World War Two, six million people, the heart of world Jewry, were killed in the Nazi Holocaust.

Central Zionist Archives

6. Immigrants from Afghanistan arriving in 1948

In 1948 the United Nations approved the end of the British Mandate and the founding of the State of Israel. Holocaust survivors came home to Israel. Jews from other countries flooded in to help build the new state. But even before the celebrations ended, the armies of five Arab countries invaded the new state to crush it at birth.

Central Zionist Archives

7. An Israeli soldier defending the road to Jerusalem during the War for Independence, 1948

Since 1948 there have been four major wars and countless battles along Israel's borders. The country must always be ready for trouble. After high school, Israeli Jewish boys and girls serve in the army for two-three years. The men go back for reserve duty until they turn fifty-five!

8. Assembling plastic chairs at the Keter plant in northern Israel

Israelis work to build their country at the same time that they fight enemy attacks. The small villages and kibbutzim that drained swamps and planted trees have grown up. Today they export oranges, cotton, apples, and other crops. Factories made thousands of products like leather coats, beach chairs, computer parts, army tanks, and brightly-colored underpants.

Arieh Stark

Dov Gubitch

9. **Ethiopian immigrants at an Independence Day party**

Israel's population had tripled since the state was established. Immigrants came from all over the world. In the last few years many immigrants from Ethiopia and Russia have been coming. The government establishes classes where they learn Hebrew and helps to provide housing, jobs, and schooling.

10. **Nahf, an Arab village in northern Israel**

One-quarter of Israel's citizens are Arab and Druze. They attend Israeli universities, vote in Israel's elections, and work beside Israeli Jews. Many Druze and a few Muslim and Christian Arabs serve in Israel's army. But many Arabs are torn by the wars between Israel and her neighbors because they have close ties of family and friendship with people in the enemy lands.

11. **Terrorism in newspaper headlines**

Israel occupied Judea, Samaria, and the Gaza Strip as a result of the Six Day War in 1967. Most of the territory's population is Arab. Historically, Judea and Samaria were the center of biblical Israel. Today many residents of the territories fight the Israelis with rock throwing and fiercer violence. There is no easy answer to the question: Whose land is this?

12. **Knesset building in Jerusalem**

The Knesset is Israel's congress. It writes the laws of the country. Knesset members are chosen from Israel's political parties. The more votes a party gets in the general election, the more members of the Knesset it chooses. The strongest party invites smaller parties to join it in forming a coalition government.

13. The Jerusalem Great Synagogue

There is no separation of church and state in Israel. Births, deaths, marriages, and divorces are supervised by the leaders of each religious community. Religious political parties are represented in the Knesset and in the government. Children may go to a secular (nonreligious) school or to the school of their religious community.

14. Nursery school at Leo Baeck, a Reform-affiliated school in Haifa

The Israeli Reform movement is small. Early Reform Jews in Europe and the United States were against building a Jewish homeland. "Jews are a religious community, not a nation," they argued. Some changed their minds after World War One. Later, with the rise of Nazism, Reform Jewish leaders like Abba Hillel Silver and Stephen Wise fought for the establishment of a Jewish state. The Reform movement's Leo Baeck School was founded in 1939. Today American student rabbis also study at Hebrew Union College in Jerusalem. NFTY kids explore Israel each summer and members of ARZA (Association of Reform Zionists of America) support Israel and Reform Judaism in Israel.

15. Picking grapes at Kibbutz Yahel

There are two Reform kibbutzim, collective settlements, in southeast Israel: Yahel and Lotan. In the north there is the village of Har Halutz. Twenty-one more Reform congregations have been formed in Israeli cities and towns. In Jerusalem the Israel Religious Action Center leads the battle for religious freedom.

Ed Toben

16. Dance festival in the park in Karmiel

Here are some favorite Israeli sports: hiking, spelunking (lots of caves to explore), dancing, basketball, skin diving, playing shesh-besh (backgammon), arguing politics, and sitting at cafes to people-watch.

Dov Gubitch

Activities

A WORD SEARCH ABOUT ISRAEL

```
A  T  K  O  T  E  L  O  O  P  S
B  H  S  Y  A  H  E  L  S  A  E
L  E  T  H  I  O  P  I  A  N  I
E  O  A  B  C  J  F  L  A  G  Z
O  D  B  U  T  E  N  A  L  L  I
B  O  B  A  T  R  E  E  S  H  O
A  R  A  B  R  U  S  S  I  A  N
E  H  K  N  E  S  S  E  T  R  I
C  E  A  R  Z  A  L  U  T  H  S
K  R  L  L  E  L  O  L  R  A  T
A  Z  Z  A  S  E  T  P  A  L  A
B  L  Y  X  W  M  A  A  N  U  U
C  L  M  N  O  P  N  N  L  T  N
R  T  S  V  N  L  P  S  B  Z  G
```

In this jumble of letters above you'll find words to match the explanations below. Circle each word you find. Keep looking across and down until you find all sixteen words.

1 Famous early Zionist leader
2 Names of two Reform kibbutzim
3 Name of Reform village in Israel
4 Language class (Hebrew word)
5 Two nationalities of new immigrants
6 Capital city of Israel
7 Israel's congress (Hebrew word)
8 Initials of Reform Zionist organization
9 There are two stripes and a star on the _____ of Israel
10 One-quarter of Israel's citizens are _____
11 Hebrew word for the "Wall" of the Temple Mount
12 Name of Reform-affiliated school in Haifa
13 The Jewish National Fund plants _____
14 A person who believes in and supports the Jewish homeland of Israel is a _____

WHAT DO *YOU* THINK?

Do you feel a connection to Israel?
If you do, how do you express the connection?
 – Parade on Israel independence Day
 – Buy JNF tree certificates
 – Write to an Israeli pen pal

   Other _____

What do you think about Israel?
 – Proud of Israel
 – Worried about Israel's security

   Other _____

Some Good Books   Adler, David. *Our Golda: The Story of Golda Meir.* New York: Viking/
                         Penguin, 1984.

                         Burstein, Chaya, M. *A Kids Catalog of Israel.* Philadelphia: Jewish Publica-
                         tion Society, 1988.

                         Cohen, Barbara. *The Secret Grove.* New York: UAHC, 1985.

                         Gurko, Miriam *Theodor Herzl: The Road to Israel.* Philadelphia: Jewish Pub-
                         lication Society, 1988.

                         Morris, Ann, and Rivlin, Lily. *When Will the Fighting Stop? A Child's View
                         of Jerusalem.* New York: Atheneum, 1990.

                         Ofek, Uriel. *Smoke over Golan: A Novel of the 1973 Yom Kippur War in
                         Israel.* New York: Harper Junior Books, 1979.

                         Semel, Nava. *Becoming Gershona.* New York: Viking/Penguin, 1990.

ADD IT ALL UP AND COLOR IT IN

Living as a Jew doesn't just happen. It takes some doing.

Doing what? That's the question this book has tried to answer.

Now that you've finished this book here's another question to answer: Why do it? Why should we be thoughtful, active Reform Jews?

In this chapter I have written and illustrated five answers that are right for me. Color those illustrations that you agree with. Then write and illustrate your own answers in the blank boxes at the end of the chapter.

Here are my answers:

1. I believe in God. That helps me to believe that I and everything else in the world have meaning and purpose, even when I don't fully understand what or why.

2. Everybody is "something" and comes from some root or background. As a Reform Jew I learn to understand my roots, my history, and my traditions.

3. I have a framework to live inside of: first, the happy framework of the yearly cycle of holidays; second, the ceremonies of the whole cycle of Jewish life from birth to death; and third, the circle of the Jewish community that lives by these customs.

4. Sooner or later I'll come up against anti-Semitism. As a thoughtful, active, knowledgeable Jew I'll be strong enough to face it. I'll respect myself, my history, and my beliefs.

5. I need to be reminded of my responsibilities to myself, to others, and to God. The standards of Torah and *mitzvot* remind me to care and to take care of others.

1.

Activities

Look up the word "Jew" in three different dictionaries. Write the definitions.

1. _____

2. _____

3. _____

List ten words that describe a "Jew" to you.

1.   5.   9.

2.   6.   10.

3.   7.

4.   8.

PUZZLE ANSWERS

Chapter 1
MATCH IT

1-10
2-9
3-7
4-6
5-4
6-5
7-8
8-3
9-2
10-1

Chapter 2
HISTORY REBUS

1. Ethiopians
2. Canaan
3. Torah

CHECK THE CORRECT BOX OR BOXES

1. the Ten Commandments
2. bring gifts to God and celebrate holidays
3. pray and study Torah in synagogues
4. adapt the Torah's laws to their changing lives
   explain the laws of the Torah more fully
5. were often persecuted and killed
   developed a strong Jewish religious framework, a *halachah*
6. an ancient section of Rome
   Jewish neighborhoods surrounded by a wall
7. freedom to leave the ghettos
8. find economic opportunities and become rich
   escape from pogroms and anti-Semitism
9. a huge, terribly destructive fire
   the murder of six million Jews by the Nazis during World War Two
10. come from all over the world
    are of different religions

Chapter 5

ABC OF REFORM JUDAISM CROSSWORD PUZZLE

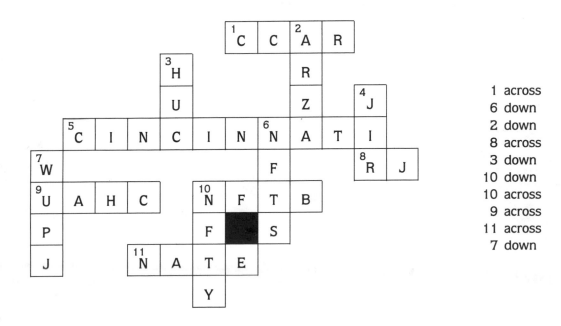

1 across
6 down
2 down
8 across
3 down
10 down
10 across
9 across
11 across
7 down

Chapter 6
CAN YOU MATCH THESE?

1-9
2-10
3-8
4-11
5-5
6-7
7-4
8-3
9-2
10-6
11-1

Chapter 9
MATCH THESE WORDS TO THEIR MEANINGS

1-8
2-13
3-9
4-12
5-2
6-11
7-5
8-4
9-7
10-1
11-3
12-6
13-10

Chapter 12
A WORD SEARCH ABOUT ISRAEL

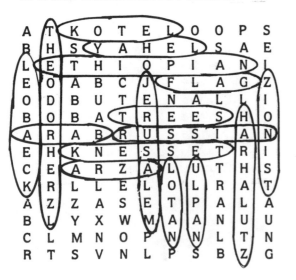

Chapter 8
CONNECT THE DOTS IN HEBREW

shofar   sukah
Rosh Hashanah   Sukot
Yom Kippur

Torah   Megillah
Simchat Torah   Purim

challah   chanukiyah
Shabbat   Chanukah

Chad Gadya   Ten Commandments
Pesach   Shavuot

Chapter 11
SPEAK HEBREW

1. boker tov בֹּקֶר טוֹב
2. yom huledet sameach יוֹם הוּלֶדֶת שָׂמֵחַ
3. lehitraot לְהִתְרָאוֹת
4. lechayim לְחַיִים
5. Shabat shalom שַׁבָּת שָׁלוֹם
6. layelah tov לַיְלָה טוֹב

HEBREW NAMES

Boys' Names	Girls' Names
Adam – 7	Alisa – 14
Alon – 25	Aviva – 19
Ami – 27	Devora – 31
Ari – 16	Dina – 17
Avi (Avraham) – 28	Elana – 30
Benjamin – 32	Naomi – 15
Daniel – 8	Nitza – 2
David – 9	Noa – 29
Dov – 22	Orli – 35
Ehud – 20	Rina – 26
Haim – 33	Rivka – 6
Joel – 10	Sharon – 4
Matan – 36	Shira – 26
Michael – 12	Shoshana – 3
Noam – 15	Tamar – 1
Ron – 11	Tova – 23
Uri – 34	Varda – 3
Ya'akov – 24	Yael – 5
Yona – 21	Yaffa – 13
Zev – 18	Yonat – 21